CRAFTING ACTIVITY AT HOME

AN UNOFFICIAL GUIDE TO HELP YOU WITH CRICUT MACHINE AND DESIGN SPACE! MANY IDEAS AND NEW PROJECTS!

ELEANOR NELSON

CONTENTS

Introduction	v
1. Buy Cheap Cricut Materials For Your Business	1
2. The Explorer 2 Model	5
3. Intermediate Projects	47
4. Advanced Projects	91
Conclusions	171

© **Copyright 2021 by Eleanor Nelson - All rights reserved.**

This document is geared towards providing exact and reliable information in regard to the topic and issue covered.

- From a Declaration of Principles which was accepted and approved equally by a Committee of the American Bar Association and a Committee of Publishers and Associations.

In no way is it legal to reproduce, duplicate, or transmit any part of this document in either electronic means or in printed format. All rights reserved.

The information provided herein is stated to be truthful and consistent, in that any liability, in terms of inattention or otherwise, by any usage or abuse of any policies, processes, or directions contained within is the solitary and utter responsibility of the recipient reader. Under no circumstances will any legal responsibility or blame be held against the publisher for any reparation, damages, or monetary loss due to the information herein, either directly or indirectly.

Respective authors own all copyrights not held by the publisher.

The information herein is offered for informational purposes solely and is universal as so. The presentation of the information is without contract or any type of guarantee assurance.

The trademarks that are used are without any consent, and the publication of the trademark is without permission or backing by the trademark owner. All trademarks and brands within this book are for clarifying purposes only and are owned by the owners themselves, not affiliated with this document.

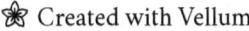 Created with Vellum

INTRODUCTION

A Cricut is a cutting system that helps you to cut and make beautiful and amazing crafts with materials that you didn't even know existed, that's the short answer. You can also sketch, emboss and produce folding lines to realize 3D designs, birthday cards, boxes, etc. depending on the layout you have.

When you have two or three projects in mind, look at your current crafting supplies. Do you have the majority of materials for one of those projects? If so, start with that one! If not, put all three projects in a hat and draw one. If you like it, do it. If you feel a pang of sadness because you drew the name of a project you really did not want, then do the one you discovered you want to do!

The Cricut machine has a number of usages in addition to being a cutter machine for a scrapbooking design. It is possible to make use of the designs to produce items like welcoming memory cards, wall surface decorations, therefore a lot more. You need to believe artistically. There are actually no borders, as well as they're all a figment of your creative imagination if there are any.

The Cricut machine is user-friendly and versatile. There is hardly a limit to what you can do with your machine, and the projects can be fun and as challenging as you want to make them.

There are plenty of decorations you can make using these machines, whether it's for Christmas, Halloween, or other seasonal-themed decorations. Perhaps you are looking for something more permanent, like unique hanging planters.

CHAPTER ONE

BUY CHEAP CRICUT MATERIALS FOR YOUR BUSINESS

SUITABLE EQUIPMENT for use with a Cricut machine.

The machines can use many different materials for any project you desire, and we will be breaking down which machine can use what materials. You should know that there are materials that the Maker can cut that the other machines cannot; as a matter of fact, they include over one hundred different types of fabric. The official website of the Cricut machines periodically upgrades, in what they say the machines can cut, so as a result, you will need to check their website often. In doing so, you will realize what you can still cut even if it may have been taken off of the list.

- Tattoo paper
- Washi tape

- Paint chips
- Wax paper
- Faux suede
- Wrapping paper
- Washi paper
- Posterboard
- Parchment paper
- Sticker paper
- Construction paper
- Photo paper
- Printable fabric
- Magnetic sheets
- Paper grocery bags
- Craft foam
- Window cling vinyl
- Cardstock
- Flannel
- Vellum
- Duck cloth
- Wool felt
- Corkboard
- Tissue paper
- Duct tape
- Matte vinyl
- Iron-on vinyl
- Leather up to 2.0 mm thick
- Sheet duct tape

- Oilcloth
- Soda cans
- Stencil film
- Glitter foam
- Metallic vellum
- Burlap
- Transparency film
- Chipboard that is up to 2.0 mm thick
- Aluminum metal that is up to .14 mm thick
- Stencil vinyl
- Glitter vinyl
- Glossy vinyl
- Denim
- Felt
- Silk
- Polyester
- Other items that the Explore Series can cut are listed below:
- Chalkboard vinyl
- White core
- Rice paper
- Photo framing mat
- Pearl cardstock
- Cereal boxes
- Freezer paper
- Iron-on
- Printable iron-on

- Glitter iron-on
- Foil iron-on
- Foil embossed paper
- Neon iron-on
- Matte iron-on
- Mesh
- Calico
- Crepe paper
- Gauze
- Interlock knit
- Terry cloth
- Velvet
- Knits

CHAPTER TWO

THE EXPLORER 2 MODEL

CRICUT IS the brand name of a company that provides a variety of different home die-cutting machines that are primarily for personal use, but many use them for commercial use. These machines are used for home projects such as scrapbooking and other creative projects such as creating personalized bags and greeting cards. The Cricut brand of die-cutting machines is popular among people who are avid paper crafters, card makers, and those who are still keeping the spirit of scrapbooking alive. These machines can be used with various materials such as cutting paper, vinyl for car blinds, iron-on for shirts, felt woods such as balsa, and thinner type woods such as those used in patterns and other various types of fabrics and materials. The Cricut logo is creative in that it is a play on the cricket bug. It is an animated bug with a happy smile that strictly refers to cricket. The logo for Cricut is easy to understand and emphasize when you see it across all different types of product offerings from the brand. These product offerings include Cricut Design Space and the new Cricut Access offering.

Cricut was introduced and empowered home crafters worldwide to do it themselves with new, fun, and more innovative designs than are currently available on the market. It was a new way for people to approach a project idea in a new and creative way. Cricut was created to provide a way to influence creative passions and bring original ideas out into the open that were once just ideas in mind with different types of materials that we can see and feel. People worldwide have created very profitable businesses where they can create personalized projects and gifts not only for their friends and families but for people all over the world who like to give a custom touch to gifts they give to their loved ones.

Now is the perfect time to join the new wave of people discovering all the different things they can do with a Cricut and for those looking to make money from it. The ideas and options of Cricut machines are limitless, but the possibilities are endless when it comes to what you can create with it once you know about it.

There are many differences between the Cricut

Expression Machine and the Cricut Explore Air 2. This is because the Cricut Expression Machine is a very old version of Cricut, and the Explore Air 2 is one of the new options available from Cricut. The Expression Machine is no longer widely available for purchase, but many people who have worked with Cricut since the early stages of the company know that they are still around for use, and many still have the machine itself. The Expression machine can still be used with the cartridges. Still, we recommend that if you have an Expression machine, you upgrade your machine to explore Air 2 so you are up to date on everything Cricut has to offer. You can also use the machine with Design Space, which is an upgraded version of the cartridges that we will give you more details on in the future. This is just one of the very obvious differences between the two different machines. Still, we will take the time in this first chapter to talk about each of the machines in detail so that you can better understand what each one is capable of doing. If you're in the market to get a Cricut machine, this should help you find out what machine fits you in projects you're trying to create right now.

CRICUT EXPRESSION MACHINES

As mentioned earlier, the Cricut Expression Machine is older in the line of Cricut die-cutting machines offered. However, it is still very popular among the Cricut crafting community. It is a well-crafted machine that is a great cutter that, when cared for, can last a very long time. Because that's what the Cricut Expression Machine is: the oldest dies cutter offerings, many people do not know where it is in the Cricut die cutter evolution line. The Cricut Expression Machine has two different versions, the original and the Expression 2. The Expression 2 came after the original Expression machine and has some really good improvements over the original Expression machines. Cricut Expression 2 comes before the Explore variants of the Cricut matrix machines. The Expression 2 machine comes before the Explore 1 machine and the Explore Air 1 and Explore Air 2 machines. The Expression machines are based solely on the ability to create images from the use of cutting cartridges. Newer versions of the Cricut cutting machines now allow you to upload your images and turn them into your cutting is.

The question is, what are the differences between the two Expression and Expression 2 computers? You might also want to know which is the best as far as what you get for the money you are spending. Honestly, it's a no-brainer that the Expression 2 is the best option to choose. The Expression 2 computer has a very large number of major improvements over the Expression 1 computer. A small group of people prefer the Expression 1 machine because it was much easier to use and is honestly the simplest machine that is still available on the market. Both of these machines cut equally well though. The

Expression 2 machine, however, is known for being much more user-friendly and gives the user the ability to be more creative than the Expression 1 machine allows users to be. The original machine has a small screen and a very large area for a keyboard that requires you to use things like overlays. Overlays allow you to discover all of the features of the machine. The machine also has dials that allow you to adjust the size of an image you are using and the amount of pressure you want to use the blade when cutting the image. The Expression 2 machine, however, has completely gotten rid of these features and now uses a more favorable way of creating images. The Expression 2 machine now uses a large full favorable LCD touch screen. This machine also comes with a stylus-like pen that helps you use the machine and all of your projects directly and entirely from this LCD screen if that is how you prefer to use it.

The addition of this LCD touch screen gives you the ability to change the size of your image quickly and easily, even allowing you to rotate and flip your images according to depending on your type of project. Plus, you don't need the keyboard overlays that were a requirement for the original Expression machine that can quickly become annoying when you're trying to get through a project promptly. This also helps you keep your workspace neat because everything is functional through the LCD screen on the machine rather than having to keep a stash of overlays on hand and find a place to keep them while you're not using them. There's nothing worse than trying to find a specific overlay for the project you're working on and not being able to find it because you've hidden it in the nearest drawer! Cricut works hard to include updates to machines that allow you to create less waste. This is just the beginning of what Cricut has to offer with Expression machine upgrades.

There are additional bonuses for the Expression 2 computer that are not included with the original Expression computer. The updated Expression 2 design also allows you to have a preview of your mat. This feature allows you to check and see what your design will look like once cut out on the mat. This also allows you to automatically make the pressure and speed for the most common materials you'll use with the machine. This means that you can select the vinyl for your project, and the machine will automatically know what amount of pressure to use to make sure it's cutting through all the material. How fast it can move through cutting the design, so you don't end up snagging the material and ruining your design. This also helps eliminate waste in materials. You're also saving time. After all, you won't have to set the pressure and speed yourself and keep starting your project over because you're at a point where you messed up your material or didn't have the right amount of pressure to cut through your material.

One of the downsides of the older Expression Machine models is that they can't allow you to load and create custom projects and images. You only can use the default cartridges or purchase the digital images that the Cricut Craft Room software has available for your personal use. This is also annoying for older models of Expression machines because if you go the cartridge route, you will have to maintain a storage space for all of your cartridges. After all, they are physical items that you need to plug into the machine use essentially. This can be very messy because having a different cartridge for each design you want can make you take up more space than your actual machine. With the inclusion of digital designs, at least you have the ability to store them on your computer, so you don't have a lot of physical cartridges lying around and causing a mess in your workspace. However, it reamends on the type of crafter you are. Many people who are still very loyal to using expression machines are not bothered by cartridges and actual them to digital designs because they are more likely to work the way you intend them to work and you. You've to deal with as many technical difficulties as you might when working strictly with digital images.

Cricut Expression 2 comes with the machine itself and two cartridges that are already preloaded with designs that you can use immediately. These cartridges include the essential Cricut designs and a cartridge for the Cricut alphabet. You'll also get a 12" by 12" cutting mat to get you started. You'll find that this mat will get the most use as it fits the needs of most projects you're likely to start with. Cricut also offers different sizes in their cutting mats, as well as viscosity levels, but we'll talk about those in the next chapter. The box will also include three different door covers to keep powder out of the spot on the machine where you'll insert the cartridges when in use.

You'll also receive an LCD screen protector, which is a great way to maintain the integrity of the LCD screen on your machine. It will also help it wear out too quickly since you will probably be using it a bit. Also, to help keep fingerprints off the LCD screen is a stylus that will be included. It's just like any other stylus you've seen for touchscreen devices. This will help you maintain the screen and make sure you hit the exact options you want with precise measurement instead of running the risk of "fat fingering," something you may not want to work within your project. The machine will also come with the blade assembly to get you started. This is important because you will need this blade to cut your projects.

You will also have a USB cable to connect your computer to the machine when using the digital images that come with the Cricut Cutting program. There is a power adapter to make sure you plug into a power outlet source since the machine is not battery-powered. Be sure not to plug into an extension cord if possible, so you don't run the risk of a fire hazard. A quick start guide and operating manual are also included in the box to make sure you set up the machine correctly, and that gives you pointers on how to do a simple project the first time using the machine right out of the box. There is very little assembly required, and you should have no problem using your machine right out of the box and initial setup!

Explore Air 2 Machine

The Cricut Explore Air 2 machine belongs to the range of newest offerings in the Cricut line of press die-cutting machines. This is the newest die-cutting machine next to the Cricut Maker machine, the latest model to be released. When you initially see the Explore Air 2 machine, you might not think it's something worth getting excited about. It's very minimalistic and laid back compared to previous versions of the

Cricut die cutters. However, when you take a closer look at the machine, you'll quickly discover that this little cutter leads the pack in the home craft cutting market. For example, this machine is perfectly designed to cut at nearly twice as fast as the machines before it, including the Expression line of machines. The Explore Air 2 machine offers the ability to cut in two different modes, the normal mode, and the fast mode. All you have to do without switching between the two modes is switch the option from one to the other. Switching to fast mode is a great option when you need to make every second working on a particular project count. This can be when you're under the gun to complete a project due to client deadlines.

A further major feature of the Explore Air 2 machine is its huge library of images all ready to use. This is the new Design Space program offered with the Explore Airline and newer, and it's all digital images rather than having to use cartridges. The Design Space program comprises over 3,000 easy-to-use designs and project ideas that are ready to go in a snap and can get you on the road to creation much faster. Depending on what you're looking for, you can use the pre-loaded images to start creating your plan, or you can use any pre-made projects where all you have to do is gather materials and tools and simply press go and let the machine do all the work for you. This option is great if you are just starting with a die-cut machine because you may not know what you can do with the machine yet.

Once you have a few projects behind you, you can start using the Design Your Project option to get even more creative. The best part about Design Space is that you won't have to pay extra for many of these projects. They're already loaded and free to use, as often as you want!

You'll also find the Explore Air 2 machine cutting edge because of its ability to sync with smart devices. That means you can use the unit with tablets, smartphones, and PCs, and they're all compatible for use with the machine and the design space because you can cut directly from your phone to the machine with the Bluetooth connection option. Being a crafter and designer means you have a lot more freedom to work out your next project when you're on the go. You have the option to save your designs within the design space without cutting them, so if an idea strikes you at any time, you can simply use the app to bring the design to life and save it for a time when you can get in front of your die cutter and create a physical representation of it. It's very simple and easy to use. This is the next level of flexibility that crafters need when you're always on the go and need to design something at a moment's notice. You'll end up sitting on the subway dreaming up new ideas to cut when you get to your destination, rather than just wondering when your ride will be over. You can simply turn on your computer and give yourself the finishing touches on a design that you can print out as soon as you get home.

Regardless of which Cricut model you choose, you simply can't go wrong with the options available. If you're more into the technological side of nesting machines, the Explore Air 2 might be the best option for you. You may want to run a hands-on project run with your computer after the initial setup is complete. This will help you understand what all the machines can do and what you must do with the machine to ensure you get what you want from it, depending on the material you are using. The Explore Air 2 machine gives you everything you need to get started with at least 1 test project, so we encourage you to take advantage of the opportunity to work with the materials and tools you are given so that you start in a position of comfort when you move on to more personal and intricate projects. We also recommend that you investigate the bundle options provided on the Cricut website so that you may begin a variety of materials and tools immediately in an affordable way. There's nothing like getting your machine and wanting to start a project, only to be reminded that you now have to go and get the materials and tools you need to make it happen.

Once you've chosen your design and gathered the materials you need, it's important to make sure the face of the machine is set to the correct material to make your cutting go smoothly. Be sure to make this part of your routine a regular one. There's nothing like cutting a very detailed design only to find out that you had it in the wrong setting, and you'll have to run it through the process to extract the desired cut. This means that if you're working with paper to make a birthday card for a friend, you'll want to make sure that the dial is set on cardstock so that it has the proper pressure for the blade to cut all the way through. There's nothing worse than cutting a card only to find that it only got halfway through! This is the same for cutting vinyl. If you're trying to create a shirt, for example, you'll want to make sure the dial is set to vinyl or vinyl + so that it's cut all the way through to remove the access vinyl from the cut image easily.

You will also need to ensure this if you are making a shirt, the option to mirror your image is turned on. This means that Design Space will automatically flip your image so that once you go to iron the design onto the shirt, it's the right orientation you want, rather than backward. If you keep your dial set to vinyl when you work on many short projects, it's great that Design Space asks you if you want to turn on the mirror option before you start a cut. It never hurts to have someone or something looking for you to make sure you cut it right the first time.

FAQ

1. Is a wireless Bluetooth adapter required for all Cricut Explore machines?

No. It is only needed for Explore and Explores One. Explore Air and Explore Air 2 have built-in Bluetooth, and therefore, there is no need for a wireless Bluetooth adapter.

1. Difference between Cricut Explore machines? The tool holder is the first difference. Explore One does not have a tool holder, which means it can cut and mark in two passes, while Explore, Explore Air, and Explore Air 2 have a dual tool holder for cutting and writing or cutting and drawing in one pass. Explore and Explore One require a Cricut wireless Bluetooth adapter to cut wirelessly from iOS, Android or computer, while Explore Air and Explore Air 2 have built-in Bluetooth.
2. Carrying Bags. You will need to purchase a

carrying bag separately. Can I write and mark with the Explore One machine? Yes, but you need to purchase the Explore One Accessory Adapter. Change this adapter to the blade housing to write or mark with the Explore One machine.
3. What about the weights and dimensions of the Explore series machine? They are similar

TROUBLESHOOTING AND FIRMWARE ISSUES

From time to time, it is necessary to troubleshoot problems with the Cricut Explore Air Machine.

Power problems

- Ensure the Cricut power cord is securely attached to the machine, adapter, and Cricut Explore wall outlet. If there is any obstruction that shakes the power cord or removes it from the wall outlet, remove it or change its Cricut machine location from the item causing the obstruction.
- Use the correct Cricut power cord and make sure the green light on the adapter box is on.
- Purchase a new Cricut power cord if you are experiencing a problem with your current one.

- Try another Cricut power cord if the one you are using is defective. If you don't have another one, purchase a new one or contact customer service for help.
- Use another wall outlet to connect the Cricut power cord to the Cricut Explore machine if the above options do not work.
- If a problem occurs after performing all of the above steps, Cricut suggests taking a video of the problem you are experiencing and contacting customer support for a solution.
- If the power button on the Cricut Explore machine is solid red and the Load Mat button is white, it means that the Cricut machine requires a firmware update. Select the upgrade option to update the firmware version.
- A power-related problem is displayed if the Power button is solid red and no other buttons are activated. Use the steps described above to correct it because the machine may not be receiving enough power.
- When powering up the Cricut Explore machine for the first time or updating the firmware and the power button is flashing or

blinking red, contact Customer Support using one of the available options.
- When loading the cutting mat onto the Cricut Explore machine and the power button flashes red, follow the steps below to resolve the problem: If the problem affects one project, the project may be damaged and require recreation, but if multiple projects are affected, go back to step 10b. It can have dirt or debris on the roller bars collected over time and, causing this error, turn off the machine, move the carriage car 3 to 4 times across the roller bar to remove the dirt. If steps 10a and 10b above do not resolve the problem, contact Customer Service for assistance.

If you are experiencing issues with the Cricut machine firmware updates failing or not running to completion, follow the steps below to resolve it:

- Make sure the Cricut machine is connected to the computer via a USB cable as using a Bluetooth connection will fail.
- Ensure that the design space on the system meets the minimum and recommended requirements.

- Disconnect the Cricut Explore machine from the computer. Turn off the computer, restart it, and reconnect to the Design Space. Try updating the firmware again and, if there is an error, proceed to the next step.
- Use a different browser to update and, if you cannot update again, go to the next step.
- Use an alternative USB cable to connect the computer to the Cricut Explore machine. If it fails to update, contact Member Support for further assistance.

Pausing while writing or scoring the project

- If the Cricut Explore computer pauses while writing or scoring the project, follow the steps below to resolve the problem:
- Close all additional open windows or tabs until the project is complete; otherwise, skip to the next step.
- Recreate the project if the problem is related to a particular project and not multiple projects. If it is related to multiple projects, skip to the next step.
- Close all computer programs running in the background and retry running the project.
- Disconnect the Cricut Explore machine from

the computer, restart the computer, and wait a moment before opening design space to continue the project.
- If everything else falls through, contact customer support at help you solve this problem.

The Cricut Explore machine catches my fabric under the roller:

- If you're facing this problem, then it's possible that your fabric extends beyond the mat's adhesive area and goes under the wide rubber roller on either side of the roller bar. To fix the problem:
- Check the size of your fabric and make sure it fits the mat properly. It should not extend outside of the adhesive region. The standard size for the FabricGrip mat adhesive area is 12 x 24 and 12 x 12.
- Use a ruler and a rotating cutter for cutting the fabric if it extends beyond the required size of the adhesive area on the mat.
- The Cricut mat becomes crooked when I load it into the Cricut Explore machine.
- The roller bar may be damaged, is loose, or uneven. Cricut recommends taking a photo

or video of the damage and contacting customer service for help. Proceed to the next step if the roller is not damaged, loose or uneven.
- Make sure you are using the correct mat size for your Cricut Explore machine. If it is the correct size, proceed to the next step.
- Make sure the mat matches the guides on the Cricut machine.
- Make sure the edge of the mat is under the roller bar.
- Apply little pressure on the Cricut mat during loading.
- Make sure the top of the Cricut mat is slightly under and against the rubber rings on the roller bars when loading the mat.
- Contact Member Services if all else fails.

The Cricut Explore machine is not able to read the sensor marks:

The reason is that the image you intend to cut is set to "Print then Cut." Change the image line to a cut line type instead of a print line if you want to cut without printing. Go to the edit bar (on Windows), the edit tool (iOS and Android) in the design space, and choose from the Line Type drop-down menu to change the line type.

If you encounter this error while running a "Print then Cut" project, follow these steps to resolve the issue:

- Make sure light sources do not interfere with the sensors on the Cricut machine. Examples include reading lamps and direct sunlight focused on the Cricut machine.
- Place all printable materials in the upper left corner of the cutting mat and apply pressure smoothly.
- Cricut recommends using white materials (81/2 "x 11") for the "Print then Cut" project because colored or patterned fabrics may affect the Cricut machine's cutting sensor.
- Use matte paper instead of glossy paper for sensor readability.
- Ensure the image fits the 6.75" x 9.25" cutting area when you do the "Print then Cut" project or try to work the size.
- Use a different browser to verify that the problem isn't coming from there.
- Use a small, dry watercolor brush to clean the cut sensor by gently sweeping it.
- Operate a computer that meets the minimum system requirements to Design Space.
- Make sure you are using the correct printer

settings. Uncheck "Reduce to Fit," "Fit Page," and other resizing options.

HOW TO MAKE THE CRICUT FAUX LEATHER BRACELET

Now we'll learn how to make leather bracelets using your Cricut Explore machine and ferrous vinyl in very simple steps.

Materials:

Cricut Explore machine, Cricut Design Space, faux leather, glue, ferrous vinyl foil, craft stick, EasyPress, chain for the bracelet.

Directions:

1. Go to Jen Goode and load the art set (four different image layouts) into your Cricut Design Space.
2. Start with the mountain design and hide any unwanted layouts. Draw and hide all the Mountain Girl pieces, leaving the mountain one behind.
3. Select the mountains and select the outline as well. Hide some cut details if you wish.
4. Create an oval shape using the Basic Shape tool, then follow it with a circle cut out of the basic shape.

5. Duplicate this layer for use on the back of the bracelet.
6. Place the vinyl foil on top of the bracelet and set EasyPress to about 250.
7. Use the glue to attach layers of faux leather, individually, of course.
8. Attach the chain and other jewelry to your bracelet. The jewelry will make your bracelet stand out.

CREATE PLANNER AND CRICUT STICKERS

Materials:

Cricut Explore Air machine, StandardGrip cutting mat, printable sticker paper

Directions:

1. Navigate to Cricut Design Space and open it.
2. Select a shape, such as square or rectangular. Alternatively, select a square, use the Unlock Dimension button to unlock its parameters, and resize it using the arrows to the desired values.
3. Use the design features mentioned above to design your shape to be filled, choose and edit the pattern, add overlays where you'll insert text, select the desired fonts to be used

to type the text on the sticker. Continue editing until you get the design you want.
4. Click the flatten button at the bottom right of the toolbar to instruct the design space to send the designed shape to the printer. Remember that you can still edit your stage sticker by clicking Deflate on the side of the sticker, edit it, and then click Flatten again. You can create multiple copies of your sticker by clicking the Duplicate button.
5. Now it's time to drop your sticker from the screen. Select the Create button in the top right corner of the screen to preview what your sticker will look like when you print it. The essence of the preview is to check that the sticker you designed you are happy with.
6. Click Continue and select Cricut Explore Air from the drop-down menu, then send it to print.
7. Select the material you want in the list of materials by clicking Browse All Materials.
8. Load your mat into your Cricut Explore machine and press the flashing Cricut button to cut the designed adhesive and pull it out finally.

HOT PAD LEATHER POTS

This is a great project idea if you have leftover leather strips from previous projects you were working on. This heating pad can help protect your home's surfaces from hot items in your kitchen and dining room. Kitchen accessories are great for people who like to spend time cooking and baking and want to bring their creative side. Many people like to purchase accessories to use in their kitchens, and it is very fun and rewarding to see their creations used in their kitchens. This project idea is great for a small housewarming gift for friends and neighbors who have just moved in or are buying homes for the first time. You can also change the color skin coloring on what you have available or match it to the colors you already show in your kitchen and dining areas.

Materials:

- Leather strips (you'll want them to be about 1 1/2 inches wide)
- Boxcutter or another type of sharp blade
- Thick string or thread
- Leather hole punch
- Need with a wide eye to fit your thick string through
- Small clamps

Provisions:

1. We recommend that you start by measuring and cutting at least eight strips of leather strips same length. For this example, you'll want to measure the length of your strips at 11 inches for the potholder. Then you'll want to weave each of the pieces together by hand. Since you have eight strips, you'll weave four across and four down. You'll weave them under and over the opposite pieces until you reach the ends. You should have excess length at the end of all sides of the potholders, but you'll want it so you can adjust it later. Don't worry about the excess material; it will be cut off later.
2. Once you have all eight pieces woven together, you'll want to use your little clamps to hold the pieces in place and together just as you need to weave them. You'll just want to clamp them together once you've put all the pieces together as tightly as possible. You'll want to do this with your hands, so you don't damage the leather you're working with.
3. Next, you'll use a hammer and nail to hit two holes that are half-inch apart on the outside edges of the square of leather created by the

weave. You'll want to make sure the hole goes through all the layers of the leather material. See below for a photo. These small holes will act as a guide for the larger holes, so this is why you want to make sure it goes through both layers in this step. One tip for this project is that you'll now want to number each strip of leather on the underside so that you can quickly put them back together after completing the next step.

4. This step is where your leather hole will come into play. Use the leather hole to drill larger holes over all the small nail holes you just created. You will need to separate all of the leather strips to do this successfully. Once you have completed this and threaded all of the larger holes over the smaller nail holes, you can put the leather strips back together. You'll want to put the leather strips back together with the same way they were before you took them apart to hit the larger holes. Then you'll want to get your long piece of string or wire. You'll use this piece of thread or twine and put it through the eye of your needle. Once it's in place, you'll pull the needle through all of the leather holes, punching holes all around the outside of the

holder or heating pad. Once complete, we recommend tying the end of the thread or string under the leather strips with a double knot or a slippy knot. Then, you can cut off the excess thread or rope once you know your knot is secure.

5. Once this is complete, take your box cutter or straight knife to trim the excess edges of the leather material on the outside of the project to create a clean look. You have the option of adding hooped string to the finished piece if you'd like the option to hang it on a hook somewhere for easy access. It's entirely up to you!

DIY EARPHONE HOLDER

This is a straightforward tutorial for making your own DIY faux leather earbud holder. This is a great learning project for someone who has experience with a sewing machine and also works great for ideas for making small gifts for friends, neighbours, or even your family members for birthdays or vacations. With the faux leather available in so many different color options, you can even pick up a neutral color that men would love, and it makes a perfect gift option for them too!

There are several different options that you can use

with this design, and it's great for anytime you want to give someone a gift to let them know you're thinking of them. Earbuds are becoming increasingly popular with teens and young adults as well, so it's a great gift idea for any person in your life that might be hard to buy! We recommend keeping this bookmarked idea to come back to later in the year when you're slammed for Christmas shopping and are looking to give more gifts this year than you are buying! Don't worry if you don't have a sewing machine; you can easily do this project with just a needle and thread, too!

In any home, it's easy to look around and find earbuds and phone cords everywhere. Cables can become a bit of a tangled mess very quickly, and earbuds are so small that they easily get missed in a sea of white cords and other Apple products in the house. If you find a way to keep all of your cables and earbuds safe and sound while still looking tidy, you'll appreciate this project. If you're not familiar with finding faux leather, Hobby Lobby or other craft stores have great options to get you started. Hobby Lobby has a section of sizeable faux leather table runners that work great for this project. They have both laser-cut and straightforward designs and work great for any project like this. If you have other faux leather lying around from previous projects, feel free to use it instead!

Materials:

- Faux leather, table runner, any color
- Magnetic sewing attachment
- The sewing machine is optional
- Needle
- String or white thread
- Scissors, the sharper, the better!
- 3x5 index card or paper you have on hand
- Sharpie
- Adhesive tape

Layout:

You'll start this project by creating a template for your earring holder. This is where your index card or thick piece of paper will come in. We recommend cutting out a two and a quarter inch by 1 1/2 inch rectangle from your index card or piece of paper. Then you will take it and cut a 1/2 inch wide strip from the same index card. You'll start by folding the rectangle in half lengthwise and cut a diagonal to create a v-shape at each end of the rectangle. Grab one piece of tape and place it to the side without a v-shaped cut and attach the half-inch wide strip of paper you cut earlier. Once completed, your template is ready to go! These cutting dimensions don't have to be exactly right. This is just a great starting point for you so that you have the correct size earbud mount. You may adjust it to enlarge it if you wish the holder to have a looser fit around the earbud case.

Next, we recommend using your permanent marker to trace the pattern onto your faux leather. We recommend using a fine-tipped sharpie so you don't have thick lines to cut when you cut the leather. Cut out the pattern on two different pieces of your faux leather simultaneously so that you have two exactly matching pieces of the pattern on your faux leather. You'll want the interiors of the leather to face each other so that the beautiful color you chose is facing out. When you have the interiors facing each other, you'll use your sewing machine or needle and thread to sew around the outer edges of the earbud holder. Once you've sewn along the entire outside of the skin, you can use scissors to cut any skin that ends up being uneven from the backing. With your needs and thread, you'll want to sew the magnetic snap so that you can close the backing around the earbuds to secure it in place. We recommend sewing the magnetic snap to the edge that is opposite the long strip of leather material. You'll want to sew on the top half of the magnetic snap at the long end of the leather material. Once you've done that, the earbud holder is complete. It's quite easy to make this earbud holder, and it's a fun project to learn how to use the faux leather material. It makes a great gift or stuffing stockings for vacations. You can change the color of the leather depending on who you are making them for. They can be quite personalized!

PAPER FLOWER GARLAND TUTORIAL

This project is a super fun way to dress up any door in your home for the changing seasons. Making garlands for your front door is always a fun project, and using your Cricut to do it now can make it even more fun. Now you can create a new wreath to update your front door for each season, or even at the beginning of each month if you wish. The possibilities are endless with the Cricut machine and the paper crafts you can create. This paper flower garland is just the beginning. You can make this project super personalized for you, as you can choose flowers that you like more than those currently in the season, depending on what time of year you plan to make your garland.

Materials:

- Colored paper, as many as you choose
- Standard Cricut Grip Mat
- Undercutting tool
- Scraper

Directions:

We suggest you start by going to Cricut Design

Space and the image section to choose the cut flower file you want. There are numerous different choices for choosing, and if you are a Cricut access user, you will have over 40,000 files to choose from that are all completely free to you. When working with flowers and cards, you'll want to maximize your space within your cardstock. You have the option to cut four large flowers at a time so that you can use as much of a 12 inch by 12-inch cardstock size as possible. Then you can use the same cut file as the flower you chose and make them smaller so that you can now fit eight smaller flowers to cut by duplicating the file on the cut to fit 4 of them per sheet. You are ready to cut once you have the flowers laid out on the card perfect in the design space. Make sure your Cricut dial is set to cardstock or cardstock + depending on how thick your paper is, and you're cut right away.

As you can see, the cut part in the entire sheet of paper before removing the paper you want to keep. Your flowers will slowly start to look like flowers once you are drawn and before you start rolling them. When you're ready to start rolling your flowers, we recommend watching video tutorials on how to do it because depending on the flower you chose, the rolling process can get complicated! Once you're done rolling your flowers, you can attach the ends with double-sided tape, and then you can attach them to your garland.

Add a little glue just to make sure your flowers are secure on your gala, and so they don't come undone.

MAKE A CARD

Here you have the opportunity to take something as simple as a card and make it into a beautiful work of art. There are different ways of doing that create a paper card with your Cricut. They may be as simple and comprehensive as you can think of! We'll start with the minimal and then apply all or just some of the techniques we know in the Design space. Creating a simple card with no design but a simple score like this is one of the easiest things to accomplish with your Cricut machine.

1. First, you'll start by adding a square and resizing it based on how big you want your card to be. You'll start by clicking on Shapes located in the left panel, so you'll want to add a square to your mat. The square that appears on your canvas area will have ides at the same length, but we'll need the sides to be different lengths to create a card. In order to do that, webtool at the resizing options on the top panel, so you'll want to click the lock between

the width and height to change each variable for different sizes. You can also unlock the proportions by selecting the square on the canvas and then clicking the lock sign located in the lower-left corner of the selection.

2. After unlocking the portions, you can resize your card to how you want it to appear. If you want to create a 5x7 inch card, you would need a 10x14 on your canvas because you will eventually fold it in half. This is a big square, and you'll need to have the 12x24 cutting mat to cut it out in one piece. You do have a card this size. You should consider making something smaller. A good size option would be a card that is five by 3.5 inches so that the size of your square would be ten by 7 inches. This is much more manageable, and you can cut it out on your 12 the 12-inch mat. When you create a square, the default fill-in color option is always gray. You may modify the color by selecting the square and then changing the fill color to white if you wish.

3. Next, you'll want to add a score line and align your card. After resizing your card to the desired size, you'll want to click on the shapes again to add the Option Scoreline. After

clicking on the dotted line, it will appear on the canvas. This line indicates that you want to create a fold line or score instead of cutting that line. You'll want to make sure you choose a score line and not a cut line because if you end up with a cut line, your Cricut machine will cut your card in half rather than create a scoreline that will help you fold it in half when your card is complete. There's a great difference between a haircut line and a scoreline, so it's worth checking and double-checking yourself before you begin the process of scoring your project with your Cricut. We recommend that you resize the line to fit the square you've already created and sized.
4. Then you'll want to select both the square and the scoring line; then, you'll want to align them by clicking the alignment option located at the top of the panel. Typically, you'll want the scoreline to be center-aligned.
5. The third step is to link the entire project together. When you link elements of a design together, you tell your Cricut that those designs are needed to go together. The colors in your project represent different materials and different mats that you will need to use

when you send your project off to be cut. Certain elements of your design, such as score lines and pen drawings, need to be assigned to a specific area where you want it to be placed. Otherwise, your Cricut will assign it to a different scoring line mat on its own. This is what happens every time you attach the scoreline and your square. You don't want this! We want to make sure both are on the same mat, just as you designed it on your canvas in Design Space. To do this, you'll need to select both elements simultaneously and simply press the Attach button in the lower right corner of the layer panel. Now, you'll be able to see your square with the scoreline attached, and even if you move the square to a different part of the mat, the scoreline will go with it.

You can also create cards from other shapes, not just squares, and rectangles. Doing so is as easy as creating one from squares and rectangles. To create a card using stars, you'll add two stars of the same size by clicking on the resize option and selecting the star. You will then select the app star, click on the Flip option, which is located in the top panel area, and select the option to flip the star upright. Overlay both of these beginnings and align them together, centered horizontally. Then you'll select the already aligned and overlapping stars and click the weld option to create the new double star shape. The welding option lies at the bottom of the seam panel. It is located on the left side of the attachment option. After welding, you will then want to add your scoreline. The scoreline will always be vertical by default. If you want to change this, you can select it and then use the rotate option in the top panel and type 90 to have a perfect horizontal scoreline. Select the welded stars and scoreline to align in the center and attach them.

If you want to have a patterned card but don't have patterned paper, you can use the Print Geometric Patterns option then Cut to make that happen. You'll need to follow similar guidelines to Print to Cut that we talked about above. To add patterns to your paper, you'll need to select it, just the paper without the scoreline. Then, for the line type, make sure you have it selected as a cut, then fill in the selection in the print option. In the Print Type window, you can select the template you want. Then you'll want to send it to your printer to print it. Take it back to your Cricut to cut it out and create the scoreline.

1. One of the coolest options you have with your Cricut machine is the ability to write

with pens. Adding text to a card will give it an extra touch of personalized love. In the last one, you learned how to create cards of different shapes. Now, we'll teach you how to write them and cut them with the Print then Cut option. You'll start by repeating the same steps you did with the star, but this time, with a heart shape. Then you'll fill it in with your favorite pattern. Like pink and white stripes, for example. Add a score line and rotate it, but don't attach it yet.

If you want to add text, click the text icon on the left side of the screen, and a box will open in the canvas area. You can type in whatever you want your card to say. Please pay attention to this next section. Within Design Space, you have system fonts and Cricut fonts. System fonts are the ones that don't have a write option. They will look like outlines when you use them within Design Space. However, in Design Space, a font has the writing capability, and you can use it to write on your paper. Typically, they cost money, but some of them are included if you have a Cricut Access subscription. Be sure to filter your fonts by those that have the writing style capability. This will ensure you use a font that will actually write on your paper and not just create the outline.

1. You also can flip and curve the text on your paper. If you want to curve the text, it is available in the top panel. You can reach the level of the desired curve by moving the slider to the left and right. If you would like to add the handwriting to the back of the paper, we recommend that you flip it vertically so it appears the right way when you fold the paper in half. After you have reversed the font correctly, you can also add a curve to it if you wish. Once you've finished the text, you'll want to select all the items within the card and attach them. Once they're attached, you'll get it done. The mat preview screen will show you how you need to put your design on the mat before it isprinting

2. For this project, you'll want it to have print, mark, design, and cut. If this is what you show, you can click Continue, and your Cricut will give you the step-by-step process. First, you're going to print it out, so you're going to send it to your printer and make sure that Cricut and the printer are connected, then press print. Then you'll set your material and move the dial, so you're on the type of material you're working with. Then you'll load your mats and the tools you

need to complete the paper. You'll be sizing, writing, and cutting the paper you just printed, so you'll need a pen, scoring stylus, and cut wheel or fine point blade. At each point, you are using a new tool. The Cricut will stop and give you time to load the tool before moving on to the next feature. Once the tool is loaded, you press C again, and the Cricut will continue with the next item in the project. Once completed, you will have your heart card to give to a loved one!

Notes:

As you can see, we have so many different ways to use paper with your Cricut machine to make various creative and custom projects. There are so many different card options that you can make, and some of them are of varying degrees of difficulty. You can create maps for any opportunity, and your friends and family will appreciate a handmade card from you, whether it's a birthday or holiday party. Paper is versatile within the Cricut world, and you'll be happy to see all the different things you can do with it. This book only gives you a couple of different projects that you can do, but always remember that Design Space comes with preloaded projects that are free to use. Many people are online willing to upload free project ideas for you to work on to be more comfortable working with paper on your own in your spare time. If you follow this chapter step by step, you should be a pro at the different paper projects you can create with your Cricut.

As mentioned earlier at the beginning of this chapter, we recommend that you start with paper projects if you are new to Cricut so that portable with the machine and the materials you can use within the most forgiving of the materials that go with the Cricut machine, but you. Still, you'll to be careful when using it because it can stick to your mat and end up ripping and tearing and ruining your project altogether. There are a vaisarious and techniques you can look up to see how there are ways to remove the paper without ruining your entire project. This will also help resist curling. Especially with thin paper, you may run into this problem. If you fold the mat away from the paper, it should help you peel it off without tearing or curling. Once you learn how to work with paper, your Cricut adventure will be in full swing!

CHAPTER THREE

INTERMEDIATE PROJECTS

PHOTO ENVELOPE LINERS

MATERIALS:

- Envelopes to address
- Cricut Pen Tool
- LightGrip cutting mat

Directions:

1. Open Cricut Design Space and create a new project.
2. Create a box the appropriate size for your envelopes.

3. Select the "Text" button in the lower left-hand corner.
4. Choose one handwriting font for a uniform look or different fonts for each line to mix it up.
5. Type your return address in the upper left-hand corner of the design.
6. Type the "to" address in the center of the design.
7. Insert your Cricut pen into the auxiliary holder of your Cricut, making sure it is secure.
8. Place your cardstock on the cutting mat.
9. Send the design to your Cricut.
10. Remove your envelope and repeat as needed.
11. Send out your "hand-lettered" envelopes!

CUSTOM TRANSPARENT POUCH

Necessary Equipment:

- A transparent pouch
- Peach and mint colored vinyl
- A cutting machine with a fine-tipped blade

Directions:

1. First, you can cut a sufficiently large strip into 2 vinyl rolls to prepare the cut. You can then use the cutting mat "Light Grip" to position the vinyl (one after the other, following the software). The vinyl is laid with the colored part up. The Cricut will cut the different elements by itself:
2. It is then necessary to peel off the carpet's vinyl, which can be done very quickly. Then, each element must be detached and carefully glued to the pouch. Then, you can rule to try to align the patterns by lines. But you can, of course, choose the distribution you want! By the way, you can decorate only one side, but it is quite possible to do both.
3. And then, we have the custom kit. It can be used as a kit to store your stationery or all those small items you tend to lose when doing crafts. Peach motifs make it almost a full-fledged decorative object. But for those who leave this summer and have planned to go to the beach or the pool, this pouch can be used to store their swimsuit, sunglasses, sunscreen... it can also simply serve as a toiletry bag or makeup.

THE CARD "ICE"

Necessary Equipment:

- 4 sheets of cardstock (Depending on the colors you want)
- A glue sticks
- A cutting machine with a fine-tipped blade

Directions:

1. To make this, you don't have to make things hard for yourself: Place at each step a sheet of cardboard paper on the cutting mat and start the machine.
2. Then just paste the whole thing. The white part serves as a "support;" it is also on its back that one can write the card's contents. It is necessary to glue the pale pink paper, then the dark pink and finally the yellow banner and the writing "ice cream." I told you: it's all simple.
3. Again, think of the several uses for this handmade card. Of course, we can write on it and send it to whoever we want. The idea of matching through postcards personally pleases me always as much. But this card can

also be merely decorative, put on a desk, a shelf, or even placed on a mood board for the summer.

SIMPLE CLOTH NAPKINS

Materials:

- Scraps of cotton fabric
- Adhesive textile vinyl (optional)

Directions:

1. The first step will be to cut two rectangles of fabric 14cm long x11cm wide with the Cricut machine.
2. When you have the pieces cut, place one on top of the other with the rights facing each other and, with a slight separation of 1cm, sew around it, leaving an open space to turn the piece over.
3. Now, flip it over, so the right side of the fabric is facing out, iron the piece, and backstitch around near the fabric's edge.
4. Now comes the creative part.
5. We are going to cut a textile vinyl with the Cricut machine to decorate our art strand.

6. Search the internet for an image that you like and save it on your computer.
7. Next, log into the Cricut Design Space platform, start a new project and upload the downloaded image. Depending on the image, you should choose the most appropriate option (simple, medium complexity, or complex).
8. If your image has a background that you want to delete, you will have to do it in the next window; if it doesn't (a checkerboard will appear), click to continue.
9. In the next window, select the option "Save as cut image" and fill in the project name and tags to make it easier to search.
10. You will have the image ready to cut it into vinyl using the corresponding mat for it.
11. Now you just have to iron it in the desired place according to the manufacturer's instructions and you will have finished this beautiful and practical makeup accessory.
12. You can sew on several and wash them by hand each time you use them, or you can pile them up and then put them in the washing machine!

HALLOWEEN SOUVENIR

Materials:

- Cricut Explore Air 2
- Cricut Spatula
- Color Plus Paper 180g A4 size BLACK
- Color Plus Paper 180g size A4 ORANGE CARTAGENA
- Color Plus Paper 180g A4 size GREEN BUENOS AIRES
- Color Plus Paper 180g A4 size
- Color Plus Paper Opaline 180g
- Cricut Red Pen
- Glue

You'll also have to download the Free File for the Explosive Halloween Boxes

Directions:

1. To start, open the file in Cricut's Design Space program and adjust it to the indicated size 50x35cm (it is marked at the top of the border surrounding the file).
2. Now, switch the internal lines to POINTING mode. This way, they will be creased and not cut.

3. However, to achieve the "blood in the eyes" effect, change the inner lines of the white part of the eye to DRAW mode.
4. Now it's time to cut. Let's start with the eyes with the effect of "blood in the eyes." Fit the Cricut Pen to the holder. To do this, press gently until you hear the CLICK!
5. So then, Cricut makes the drawings and then the cut! A maximum advantage, right? Yea, I know!!!
6. After the drawing is done, replace the pen with the crease tool, as we will start cutting the box!

Cut and Crease at Cricut:

Anyway, with all the pieces cut, it's time to assemble. And I'm going to warn you: It's so easy to do! Now is the time to call the kids to participate!

1. Let's start by gluing the seam part to complete the box. After that, just double it!
2. Fold in the creased part of the box. At the bottom (at the base of the box), we do not glue anything else! Since this is what will give the explosion effect when we remove the cap!
3. After that, fold the lid part and glue the sides.
4. Attach the lid to the box to start decorating. It

is essential to fit in to see how high the eyes will be.
5. Creed! That bloody eye is scary! Let's put it in place!
6. Glue your eyes and mouth ...
7. Ehmm!!! But something seems to be missing? Do you know what? Of course! The screws! Have you seen Frankenstein without a screw? Fold and glue the screw parts!
8. Then, just join these two parts! Glue the screws to the cover! And ready!!!!

Just see how easy it is to make this explosive Frankenstein box. It is ready to be filled with treats. The only certainty is that the kids will love it.

CUSTOM PILLOWS

Materials:

- Cricut Explore Air 2
- Light or Standard cutting base
- Easy Press + application base or iron
- Bright Pad
- Sewing machine
- Cricut circular cutter and fabric scissors
- Cricut Hook

- Regenerative cutting base
- Ruler
- Transfer to Cricut fabric
- Printed and white fabric 100% cotton
- Pompom or other finish - or nothing if you prefer!
- Padding
- Pins, clips and sewing thread

For many, one burning question begging for answers when completing their craft is: "Can I use my iron instead of Easy Press?"

Of course, you can. The whole point here is the efficiency of the equipment. Unlike iron, Easy Press was created for this job so it applies to the transfer perfectly.

Directions:

1. The first part of every project is the art or design that will be cut. So, the most certain thing is to start with that part. Most people prefer to use an already-saved image file. All that is left is to fixate them inside the Design Space to cut.

How to Open Image in Design Space:

1. With the program open, click Upload and choose an image to upload to the program.
2. Right after that, you will define what type of image you are uploading. You can choose between Simple (for flat core images), Moderately Complex (with more details and various colors) and Complex (with gradients and textures).
3. Click Continue, and on the next screen, you will be able to make some edits such as deleting the background of the image or even some part of the drawing. When you're the way you want, just save.
4. Now, open this image in Canvas and start by defining the size of the image you will crop. To do this, select all the parts of your image and group to work all at once safely.
5. To define the size, you can use the blue circle in the lower right corner of the image selection box or place the tool's measurements on the top bar.

JAM JAR LABELS

Materials:

- Adhesive Vinyl

- Weeding Tool
- Transfer Tape
- Jam Jars

Directions:

1. You need to prep your jars by cleaning them thoroughly. This will ensure the vinyl sticks properly. It is also important to measure the size of your jam jars; this is the height and width you have available for your Cricut labels.
2. Go into Design Space. You'll probably find that the jam or spice name you need is already there. Of course, you can design your own or use images instead. Select the image you desire, then select the detach option in actions. This prevents Cricut from relocating the name to where it will fit best when printed.
3. Don't forget to select your preferred font and resize the letters to your desired size.
4. Once you have all the names and images laid out, you can go back into the actions tab and select attach. This will lock them into the position you have chosen.

5. You can now send the file to your Cricut machine.
6. Use your weeding tool to get perfect edges as you remove all the words from the vinyl. Once you are happy with how they look, apply the transfer tape and slowly peel the backing off.
7. The transfer tape will hold it in place as you stick the letters to your clean jam jars. Once they are stuck, you can remove the transfer tape and congratulate yourself on some fine-looking jam jar labels.

THE CHORE CHART

Materials:

- Metal Board
- Cricut chore chart cartridge. This is not essential but will make it easier.
- Magnets
- Adhesive vinyl
- Transfer Tape

Directions:

1. The first thing you need to do is verify that your magnets stick to your metal board! You can then measure the surface area of your magnets; this is the size your print will need to be.
2. It is also important to make sure the magnets are clean and ready for the adhesive vinyl.
3. The next step is to go into Design Space and look at the different images available. You'll need to select an image for every chore that you or your child is likely to do.
4. Position them carefully on the screen to optimize your use of your adhesive vinyl.
5. Don't forget to create a name in Vinyl. You can use Design Space to make individual letters or join the name together.
6. Once this is done, you will need to print it all onto your vinyl.
7. Carefully remove all the letters and images. It is likely that the weeding tool will be useful at this stage.
8. Take your time as one slip can destroy your efforts!
9. Stick the transfer tape to the front of all the letters and images. Then peel the adhesive backing off and stick the vinyl images to the front of the magnets. Make sure there are no

bubbles in the vinyl before you remove the transfer tape.

Now you just need to introduce the concept to your child(ren)!

DRINKS COASTERS

Materials:

- Cork
- Adhesive Vinyl
- Adhesive Felt
- Transfer Tape

Directions:

1. Decide how many coasters you would like to make; how big they should be and what shape you want them to be. They do not need to be circular! A star, square, or even an irregular shape can be just as effective!
2. Create this shape in your Design Space and allow the Cricut machine to cut your design into the cork (max 2mm thick). If yours is thicker, then you need to cut it using a sharpie.

3. Now, you need to select the image you wish to print on each coaster. You can even choose different ones for each coaster.
4. Instead of an image, you can opt for a monogram or even a phrase or date that reminds you of a special occasion.
5. These will need to be the same size as your coaster.
6. Use the Cricut machine to cut these shapes into the adhesive vinyl. This can then be transferred to the cork using transfer tape; as described previously.
7. Make sure there are no bubbles in your vinyl as you apply it.
8. You can now add felt to the bottom to help protect your furniture or even add small pieces of felt to the top; to improve the look.
9. This step is not essential, it will depend on your design and whether you feel felt is beneficial to help protect your furniture.

BABY BLANKET

Materials:

- Cricut machine
- Iron

- Iron-on fabric
- Standard cotton fabric or plain blanket—any color

Directions:

1. Go into the Design Space app and select the numbers or tests you wish to add to your blanket. You'll need to remove any negative spaces and reverse the letters and numbers. This is so that when they are stuck to your blanket they can be read properly.
2. You can choose a date of birth, a short phrase, or even a picture. There is practically no limit to how many shapes you can create; as long as they'll fit on the blanket.
3. Now you need to use your Cricut machine to print and cut each letter and number onto your iron-on fabric. These should be ready to use as soon as they are printed.
4. You can then place them on your blanket and iron them into position.
5. The key here is to have a flat surface and then place a folded towel onto it. The blanket can go on top. This will allow your fabric to have a little flex which will ensure the edge of the images is stuck properly.

6. When ironing on the fabric, you need to ensure the temperature is at least 305°F (150°C). Hold the iron over the image for approximately 30 seconds to ensure it sticks properly.

A BOOKMARK

Materials:

- Vinyl
- Paper or card

Directions:

1. Open your Design Space and create a new shape. It is best to start with a rectangle approximately 6-inches tall by 1.5-inches wide.
2. Inside this rectangle, you'll need to place your text. You can write any short phrase you want or even add a picture.
3. Go into the settings and make sure that the text is set as a separate layer and then click attach. You can then send the file to your machine and it will cut the phrase out of your vinyl rectangle.

4. The result is a stylish bookmark with the words cut into it. It's that simple!
5. It is a good idea to then laminate the bookmarks as this will protect them and help them to last longer.

CHRISTMAS TREE ORNAMENTS

Materials:

- Cricut Machine
- Clear Plastic Ornamentation
- White Craft Paint (for better performance, suggest this brand in Wedding Cake color)
- Ribbon
- Vinyl Decals
- Transfer tape
- Weeder
- Scrapper

Directions:

1. Cover the decorations with white paint and tap softly before white paint is covered on the bottom. Don't pour too much ornament paint inside! When creating these ornaments, this is the dilemma I've learned most people

have. Within, they place way too much color, so it spills or never dries. If you think you put too much paint inside, switch the ornaments over and let them drip out until there is no stripping paint inside on a safe surface.
2. Replace the top of the ornament with the rear.
3. If you have purchased the decals from my store, build and cut the Cricut Images or skip this step.
4. Weed the vinyl off and apply the design.
5. Apply Ribbon and it's ready.

PRINT SOCKS

Materials:

- Socks
- Heat transfer vinyl
- Cutting mat
- Scrap cardboard
- Weeding tool or pick
- Cricut EasyPress or iron

Directions:

1. Open Cricut Design Space and create a new project.
2. Select the "Image" button in the lower left-hand corner and search "paw prints."
3. Select the paw prints of your choice and click "Insert."
4. Place the iron-on material on the mat.
5. Send the design to the Cricut.
6. Use the weeding tool or pick to remove excess material.
7. Remove the material from the mat.
8. Fit the scrap cardboard inside of the socks.
9. Place the iron-on material on the bottom of the socks.
10. Use the EasyPress to adhere it to the iron-on material.
11. After cooling, remove the cardboard from the socks.
12. Wear your cute paw print socks!

XMAS DECORATION

Materials:

- Cricut machine
- Cricut glitter vinyl
- Transfer tape

- Scraper tool
- Weeding tool
- Ribbon

Directions:

1. Log in to the Cricut Design Space and start a new project.
2. Click on the Input icon.
3. Type in your Christmas greetings.
4. Change the text font.
5. Ungroup and adjust the spacing.
6. Highlight and "weld" to design the overlapping letters.
7. Select the parts of the text you do not want as part of the final cut.
8. Readjust the text size.
9. Select the file as a cut file. You will get to preview the design as a cut file.
10. Approve the cut file.
11. The text is ready to cut.
12. Place the vinyl on the cutting mat shiny side down.
13. Load the mat into the machine.
14. Custom dial to vinyl.
15. Cut the image.

16. Use the weeding tool to remove excess vinyl after the image is cut.
17. Apply a layer of transfer tape to the top of the cut vinyl.
18. Peel back the vinyl paperback.
19. Apply the vinyl onto the glass ornament.
20. Go over the applied vinyl with a scraper tool to remove the air bubble underneath the vinyl.
21. Slowly peel away the transfer tape from the glass ornament.

A TABLE LAMP

Materials:

- Set of 6 Scrapbooking paper sheets—Tropical Paradise
- Slate scrapbooking sheet—Mahé, 30x30cm
- Sheet of 34 epoxy stickers—Tropical Paradise
- 8 card stock polaroid frames—Tropical Paradise
- 100m two-tone spool—Sky blue
- 16 mini clothespins 35 mm
- Vivaldi smooth sheet A4 240g—Canson - white n° 1
- Precision cutter and 3 blades

- Blue cutting mat—2mm, A3
- Black acrylic and aluminum ruler 30cm
- Precision scissors 13.5cm blue bi-material rings
- 3D adhesive squares
- Pack of 6 HB graphite pencils

Directions:

1. Gather the materials.
2. Using the template and a pencil, reproduce the palm tree on the papers in the collection.
3. Cut out with a cutter or scissors.
4. Assemble the trunk of the palm tree. Glue the foliage. Using the template, reproduce the traces of the cocktail support on thin cardboard, following the dimensions indicated. Cover it with the collection paper.
5. After having cut in the slate sheet: 1x (8.5x8.5 cm), choose a Polaroid. Glue the slate sheet to the back of the Polaroid. Using a chalk pen, write "Cocktail of the day." Decorate with the stickers. Fold the support at the dotted lines.
6. Using the templates and a pencil, draw the leaves and flowers on the Mahé paper and on the collection paper. Draw.

7. Choose photos. Cut them to size: 8.5x8.5 cm. Stick to the back of the Polaroids.
8. Glue the leaves and flowers together. Cut the string to the desired dimensions and glue it to the back of the flowers. Glue the birds on the string and hang the photos using mini clips.
9. And here is a pretty summer and tropical decoration! Beautiful evenings in perspective.

LUGGAGE TAGS

Materials:

- Cricut Faux Suede or other substantial material of your decision
- Cricut Pen
- Shower Adhesive
- Cowhide line
- Cricut Explore Air, Cricut Explore Air 2, or Cricut Maker
- Solid Grip Cutting Mat

Directions:

1. This project is in fact a Make It Now project in the Cricut Design Space, however, in the

event that you go directly there, you can't tweak it with your name and contact data. So all things considered, click the Images tab in the left sidebar and quest for "gear tag."
2. Look down until you discover this gear tag and addition it to your canvas. You'll see that there's space to include your own content over the plane on the rear of the tag.
3. Change the textual style by utilizing the drop-down menu on the correct side. You can sort by "expressing" style to discover the text styles that work with the pen instrument.
4. When you have put your name, select everything on your canvas and snap "attach." This guarantees your contact data writes in the right spot on your gear tag.
5. Hit Make It and follow the on-screen prompts to compose and cut your baggage tag! Utilize splash glue to stick the two sorts out and bind to your pack with a cowhide rope or other strip on the cording! Such a simple undertaking that will assist you with monitoring your bags when you travel.

COLORING PAGES

Materials:

- White Kraft paper or a big sheet of white paper
- Cricut Explore or Maker
- Cricut Pens
- 1224 mat

Directions:

1. Open Design Space and pick your design, to begin with. I searched for "draw Christmas" and chose these adorable woodland creatures, ideal for drawing with pens.
2. Once I had about a 12x12 section filled with animals and holly, I hit CTRL+A to select everything and copy and paste the entire design below. It saved me much work, not having to move and replace each object.
3. Hit the Make It button once you have everything in location. The software reminds you need a larger mat since your project is larger than 11.5x11.5".
4. Now comes the fun part: wait. The black will take at least an hour, but I didn't. You can

switch the pen, get the quick parts out of the way, and do something else while Cricut draws the designs.
5. Once finished, remove it thoroughly and wrap your gift.

WOODEN SIGN

Materials:

- Acrylic paint for whatever colors you would like
- Vinyl
- Cricut Explore Air 2
- Walnut hollow basswood planks
- Transfer Tape
- Scraper
- An SVG file or font that you wish to use
- Pencil
- Eraser

Directions:

1. You will need to start by deciding what you will want to draw onto the wood.
2. Then, place some lines on the plank to

designate the horizontal and vertical axis for the grid. Set this aside for later.
3. Upload the file that you wish to use to the Design Space. Then, cut the file with the proper blade.
4. Weed out the writing or Design Spaces that are not meant to go on the wood.
5. Using the transfer tape, apply the tape to the top of the vinyl and smooth it out. Using the scraper and the corner of the transfer paper, slowly peel the backing off a bit at a time. Do it carefully.
6. Remove the backing of the vinyl pieces, aligning the lettering or design so that it is fully centered. Place it carefully on the wooden plank.
7. Again, use the scraper to smooth out the vinyl on the plank.
8. Take off the transfer tape by smoothing off the bubbles as you scrape along with the wood sign. Discard the transfer tape at that time.
9. Continue to use the scraper to make the vinyl smoother. There should be no bumps since this creates bleeding.
10. Now, paint your wood plank with any color of your choice. Peel the vinyl letters off. Once

the paint has completely dried, you are able to erase your pencil marks.

SNOWMAN LANTERN

Materials:

- Cricut Maker or Cricut Explore
- Standard Grip mat
- Vinyl in desired colors
- Transfer tape
- Scraper
- Weeder
- Glass etching cream
- Glass faced lantern

Directions:

1. Log into the "Design Space" application and click on the "New Project" button on the top right corner of the screen to view a blank canvas.
2. Click on the "Projects" icon and type in "Snowman Lantern" in the search bar.
3. Click on "Customize" to further edit the project to your preference or simply click on the "Make It" button, and load the vinyl sheet

to your Cricut machine and follow the directions on the screen to cut your project.
4. Using a weeder tool, remove the negative space pieces of the design.
5. Use the transfer tape to apply the vinyl cuts to the glass face of the lantern.
6. Then use the scraper tool on top of the transfer tape to remove any bubbles and then just peel off the transfer tape.
7. Lastly, apply the etching cream following the directions on its package, and rinse off to remove the vinyl.

UNICORN WINE GLASS

Materials:

- Stemless wine glasses
- Outdoor vinyl in the color of your choice
- Vinyl transfer tape
- Cutting mat
- Weeding tool or pick
- Extra fine glitter in the color of your choice
- Mod Podge

Directions:

1. Open Cricut Design Space and create a new project.
2. Select the "Text" button in the Design Panel.
3. Type "It's not drinking alone if my unicorn is here."
4. Using the dropdown box, select your favorite font.
5. Adjust the positioning of the letters, rotating some to give a whimsical look.
6. Select the "Image" button on the Design Panel and search for "unicorn."
7. Select your favorite unicorn and click "Insert," then arrange your design how you want it on the glass.
8. Place your vinyl on the cutting mat, making sure it is smooth and making full contact.
9. Send the design to your Cricut.
10. Use a weeding tool or pick to remove the excess vinyl from the design. Use the Cricut Bright Pad to help if you have one.
11. Apply transfer tape to the design, pressing firmly, and making sure there are no bubbles.
12. Remove the paper backing and apply the words to the glass where you'd like them. Leave at least a couple of inches at the bottom for the glitter.

13. Smooth down the design and carefully remove the transfer tape.
14. Coat the bottom of the glass in Mod Podge, wherever you would like glitter to be. Give the area a wavy edge.
15. Sprinkle glitter over the Mod Podge, working quickly before it dries.
16. Add another layer of Mod Podge and glitter and set it aside to dry.
17. Cover the glitter in a thick coat of Mod Podge.
18. Allow the glass to cure for at least 48 hours.
19. Enjoy drinking from your unicorn wine glass!

LEATHER KEYCHAIN

Materials:

- Cricut Iron-on Foil in rose gold
- Cricut EasyPress 2 Small
- Cricut EasyPress Mat
- Cricut True Control Knife
- Keychain Lanyards
- Cricut Normal and Strong Grip Cutting
- Cricut Self-Healing
- Cricut EasyPress 2 Small

- Cricut EasyPress

Directions:

1. Start by opening up Cricut Design Space.
2. Design Space comes complete with many fonts, pictures and characteristics so that it can be used immediately after you plug into it. You can easily upload your own images, but the project today will only use a Cricut fountain.
3. Create and open a textbox to a new canvas. Specify your name, and in the drop-down list, select the ZOO DAY font. The all-caps fonts are perfect for this. It works great. When the name has been written down, the letter space is decreased so that the letters start to touch each other. Touch them before and after each letter.
4. You can check out my project here, but your own custom names must be created.
5. Make it visible to both layers.
6. Changing the iron-on vinyl color from the top layer to the color... or closing.
7. Double every name now.
8. The background of one version must be visible, the other the front.

9. Select and solder every single name. All letters will be merged into one solid piece.
10. After soldering, the background is solid and each name is solid. Choose and sweat or join all the blue names. Repeat the yellow names soldering.
11. Click on the button to make it.
12. On two separate mats, you will bring up the sold or attached words.
13. Mirror the front-end mat picture. Then, with a glittering side, place the iron-on vinyl on your mat. Set the Iron-on Foil configuration of the machine.
14. Click on the "C" button and insert it into the Cricut Maker. It will cut the picture with the fine point blade beautifully.
15. Remove the iron-on vinyl and trim the edges once cut. Set it above your Bright Pad Cricut and see where you should weed. It has a breeze. To remove excess vinyl, use the weeding tool.
16. Get the leather ready for the second mat. Leather cutting was never so easy with the Blade and the Builder Knife.
17. To help protect your cutting mat against leather, use contact paper. Remove the leather packaging and turn it roughly onto it.

18. Place the paper and securely paste it on clear contact paper. Cut the leather in plastic.
19. Slide onto the machine and put the chrome blade in the machine to the right.
20. Make certain you have calibrated the blade beforehand.
21. Put the leather-covered contact paper right on the strong grip mat.
22. Place the blade in the Cricut Maker and have a chrome blade easily cut the leather.

CREPE PAPER BOUQUET

Materials:

- Cricut Maker" or "Cricut Explore"
- StandardGrip mat
- Crepe paper in desired colors
- Floral wire, floral tape, hot glue
- Fern fronds
- Vase

Detections:

1. Log into the "Design Space" application and click on the "New Project" button on the top

right corner of the screen to view a blank canvas.
2. Let's use an already-existing project from the "Cricut" library and customize it. So click on the "Projects" icon and type in "crepe bouquet" in the search bar.
3. Click on "Customize" so you can further edit the project to your preference or simply click on the "Make It" button and load the crepe paper to your "Cricut" machine and follow the instructions on the screen to cut your project.
4. To assemble the design, follow the assembly instructions provided under the "Assemble" unit of the project details.

LEAF BANNER

Materials:

- Cricut Maker" or "Cricut Explore"
- StandardGrip mat
- Watercolor paper and paint
- Felt balls
- Needle
- Thread
- Hot glue

Directions:

1. Log into the "Design Space" application and click on the "New Project" button on the top right corner of the screen to view a blank canvas.
2. Let's use an already-existing project from the "Cricut" library and customize it. So click on the "Projects" icon and type in "leaf banner" in the search bar.
3. Click on "Customize" so you can further edit the project to your preference or simply click on the "Make It" button and load the watercolor paper to your "Cricut" machine and follow the instructions on the screen to cut your project.
4. Use watercolors to paint the leaves and let them dry completely. Then create a garland using the needle and thread through the felt balls and sticking the leaves to the garland with hot glue, as shown in the picture below.

PAPER PINWHEELS

Materials:

- Cricut Maker" or "Cricut Explore"

- StandardGrip mat
- Patterned cardstock in desired colors
- Embellishments
- Paper straws
- Hot glue

Directions:

1. Log into the "Design Space" application and click on the "New Project" button on the top right corner of the screen to view a blank canvas.
2. Let's use an already existing project from the "Cricut" library and customize it. So click on the "Projects" icon and type in "paper pinwheel" in the search bar.
3. Click on "Customize" to edit the project to your preference further or simply click on the "Make It" button and load the cardstock to your "Cricut" machine and follow the instructions on the screen to cut your project.
4. Using hot glue, adhere the pinwheels together to the paper straws and the embellishment, as shown in the picture below.

PAPER LOLLIPOPS

Materials:

- Cricut Maker or Cricut Explore
- LightGrip mat
- Patterned cardstock in desired colors
- Glitter
- Wooden Dowels
- Hot Glue

Directions:

1. Log into the "Design Space" application and click on the "New Project" button on the top right corner of the screen to view a blank canvas.
2. Let us use an already existing project from the "Cricut Library" and customize it. So click on the "Projects" icon and type in "Paper Lollipop" in the search bar.
3. Click on "Customize" to further edit the project to your preference, or simply click on the "Make It" button and load the cardstock to your Cricut machine and follow the instructions on the screen to cut your project.
4. Using hot glue, adhere the down between the

lollipop circles. Brush them with craft glue and sprinkle with glitter.

PAPER LUMINARY

Materials:

- Cricut Maker or Cricut Explore
- StandardGrip Mat
- Shimmer paper sampler
- Weeder
- Spray adhesive
- Frosted Glass Luminary

Directions:

1. Log into the "Design Space" application and click on the "New Project" button on the top right corner of the screen to view a blank canvas.
2. Let us use an already-existing project from the "Cricut Library" and customize it. So click on the "Projects" icon and type in "Paper Luminary" in the search bar.
3. Click on "Customize" to further edit the project to your preference, or simply click on the "Make It" button and load the shimmer

paper to your Cricut machine and follow the instructions on the screen to cut your project.
4. Cut and weed the design, then spray the back of the shimmer paper with spray adhesive and adhere to the glass luminary, as shown in the picture below.

PAPER BOUTONNIERE

Materials:

- Cricut
- Set of 6 Scrapbooking paper sheets
- Leaf—30.5x30.5cm, petrol blue
- Leaf—30.5x30.5cm, menthol green
- Leaf—30.5x30.5cm, lime green
- Leaf—30.5x30.5cm, spring green
- Slate scrapbooking sheet—30x30cm
- Sheet of 34 epoxy stickers
- 8 card stock polaroid frames
- Assortment of 40 die-cuts
- 100m two-tone spool—Sky blue
- 16 mini clothespins—35mm
- Vivaldi smooth sheet A4 240g—Canson, white n° 1
- Precision cutter and 3 blades
- Blue cutting mat—2mm, A3

- Acrylic and aluminum ruler 30cm black
- Precision scissors 13.5cm blue bi-material rings
- 3D adhesive squares
- Mahé Tools—scrapbooking
- Pack of 6 HB graphite pencils
- Techniques: Stencil, Collage, Origami - Folding, Tropical

Directions:

1. Discover below all the steps to realize your summer decoration "Tropical Paradise":
2. Gather the materials.
3. Using the template and a pencil, reproduce the palm tree on the papers in the collection.
4. Cut out using Cricut.
5. Assemble the trunk of the palm tree. Glue the foliage. Using the template, reproduce the traces of the cocktail support on thin cardboard, following the dimensions indicated. Cover it with the collection paper.
6. After having cut in the slate sheet: 1x (8.5x8.5 cm), choose a Polaroid. Glue the slate sheet to the back of the Polaroid. Using a chalk pen, write "Cocktail of the day." Decorate with the stickers. Fold the support at the dotted lines.

7. Using the templates and a pencil, draw the leaves and flowers on the paper and on the collection paper. Draw.
8. Choose photos. Cut them to size: 8.5x8.5 cm. Stick to the back of the Polaroids.
9. Glue the leaves and flowers together. Cut the string to the desired dimensions and glue it to the back of the flowers. Glue the birds on the string and hang the photos using mini clips.
10. And here is a pretty summer and tropical decoration! Beautiful evenings in perspective!

CHAPTER FOUR

ADVANCED PROJECTS

WINDOW STICKERS

MATERIALS:

- Cricut Explore Air (used is a good solution if you want to save some money)
- 2 Premium Outdoor Glossy Vinyl
- Transfer Tape
- Scraper Tool

Directions:

1. You can use Premium Outdoor Glossy Vinyl to transform any cut picture into a window decal. If you want, you can select a photo

from Cricut Design Space, but I'll explain how to upload an image and generate your cut file. To find the ideal picture, simply google search. There are loads of images to choose from, but the simpler the model, the faster it transfers to a cut file.

2. When you discover your picture, right-click to save it to your laptop. Go to Cricut Design Space, click New Project.
3. Click the Upload button situated at the bottom left.
4. Click Upload Image to drag or drop the picture to the next page.
5. Click the Cricut Design Space Upload button to pick your picture type. You can go simple or have fun with the colors; there are a lot of possibilities to choose from.
6. Simply click when selecting the picture type in the Cricut Design Space and choose now which picture regions are not part of the final cut.
7. Select the picture area to be cut by the Cricut machine to generate the window decal, then select the picture you have chosen.
8. This also provides you a preview of how the cut picture looks.

9. There is a back button that you can press to adjust to the image before moving forward.
10. After approving, you are taken back to the initial upload screen, but this time you can see your latest cut file among the pictures.
11. Cut your Cricut Machine Vinyl Decal. Click the picture to highlight, then select Insert Image.
12. To create your vehicle decals, select the picture to put it into the canvas. That brings the picture to your design region, where you can adjust the image's size or direction.
13. Apply carefully vinyl transfer paper decal to the window where you want to put the sticker. Then go over again with rubbing alcohol to remove surplus grease or fingerprint smudges.
14. Carefully peel back the vinyl's paperback to allow all elements of the picture release from the sheet.
15. Remove the paper backing from the car window decal to apply the vinyl, begin at one end or corner and roll the plastic down.

BABY NAPKIN

Materials:

- Cricut Machine
- Cricut EasyPress or Iron
- 23 sheets press on
- 1¼ yard white bandage texture
- Cricut Configuration Space document
- Autumn in November textual style

Directions:

1. When utilizing Cricut Press On, it's imperative to make sure to reflect the picture. You'll put it glossy side down on the tangle and cut utilizing the iron-on setting. Try not to utilize the HTV setting with your Maker. For reasons unknown, it is slicing through. You simply need it to cut the vinyl and keep the transporter sheet unblemished.
2. You'll eliminate all the negative space and after that cut every month's number with the goal that you can space them on your cover. When utilizing the Cricut EasyPress, you require a hard surface and afterward a collapsed towel on that hard surface. You

require something that will give a little with the goal that every one of the edges will be safely followed. You know you've got an awesome grip when you can see the material's surface.
3. For Iron-On Lite, you'll require a temperature of 305°F and afterward press for 2530 seconds. Give your things a decent warm-up in advance and after you're finished squeezing, turn your material over and press again for a couple of more seconds.
4. Now you're finished. So super simple yet it requires a tad of investment to get your numbers equitably dispersed and to complete the edges of your material. You'll never need to spend $40+ on a Milestone infant cover again.

SHOE DECALS

Materials:

- Shoes to embellish 1¼ Canvas are not necessary unless you want to iron on something to the top
- Adhesive vinyl or iron-vinyl, depending on your design and shoe

- Transfer tape and scraper tool
- Iron if required for iron-on

Directions:

1. In Design Space, create your image or phrase and send the file to cut out of the vinyl. You can use the phrase for one shoe and the negative vinyl for the other, or you can send the file to cut two times.
2. Use the transfer tape to remove the vinyl design and line it up on the shoe where you want to put it. Using the scraper tool, smooth the vinyl onto the shoe. If you are adding an iron-on design, heat your iron and place your vinyl on the canvas portion of the shoe. Place a cloth over the top and iron it on.
3. Peel away the backing of the vinyl, making sure it has completely attached to the shoe. You can go back over your vinyl with the iron or scraper tool to make sure everything is securely in place.

Throw on your new custom shoes and show them off to the world!

LEFTOVER BOXES

Materials:

- Sticker paper for labels or stickers
- Cardstock
- Hot glue gun or glue dots

Directions:

1. If you are going to add labels of stickers to your boxes, design them in Design Space with the image or text that you prefer. Consider adding the title of the event and the date to the label so guests know right away how long they have the leftovers in their fridge. Create a variety of sizes so they will fit over the cardstock boxes you are about to create or other containers you might need to use.
2. Once your stickers or labels are created, send the file to print and cut.
3. Search in the Design Space library the template for Chinese Take Out Boxes and load it into a new workspace. Choose a variety of sizes. Load your cardstock onto your cutting mats and send the file to cut.

4. Fold your cut cardstock along the score lines. Apply glue along the edges to assemble the box and reinforce the seams.
5. If you are adding stickers to your boxes, add them now. For other containers, keep the stickers nearby or apply them onto them as well. You are ready to send your guests away in style now!

CUSTOM COASTERS

Materials:

- Free Pattern Templates
- Monogram Design (in Design Space)
- Cardstock or Printing Paper
- Butcher Paper
- Lint-free towel
- Round Coaster Blanks
- LightGrip Mat
- EasyPress 2 (6"x7" recommended)
- EasyPress Mat
- Infusible Ink Pens
- Heat Resistant Tape
- Cricut Bright Pad (optional) for easier tracing)

Directions:

1. In Cricut Design Space, open the monogram design. You can click "Customize" and choose the designs that you want to cut out or just go ahead and cut out all the letters.
2. Click on "Make It."
3. On the page displayed, click on "Mirror Image" to make the image mirrored. This must be done whenever you are using infusible ink. For your material, choose "Cardstock." Then, place your cardstock on the mat and load it into the machine; then press the "Cut" button on the Cricut machine.
4. After the Cricut machine is done cutting, unload it, and remove the done monograms from the mat.
5. Trace the designs onto the cut-out. If you have a Cricut Bright Pad, you can use it to carry out this step much more easily, as it will make the trace lines easier to identify. Tracing should be done using Cricut Infusible Ink Pens.
6. Use the lint-free towel to wipe the coaster. Ensure that no residue is left behind to

prevent any marks from being left on the blank.
7. Make the design centered on the face-down coaster.
8. Get a piece of butcher paper that is about an inch larger on each side of the coaster and place it on top of the design.
9. Tape this butcher paper onto the coaster using heat-resistant tape, to hold the design fast.
10. Set the temperature of your EasyPress to 400°F and set the timer to 240 seconds.
11. Place another butcher paper piece on your EasyPress mat, set the coaster on top of it, face up.
12. Place another piece of butcher paper on top of these. Place the already preheated EasyPress on top of the coaster and start the timer.
13. Lightly hold the EasyPress in place (without moving) or leave it in place right on the coaster—if on a perfectly flat surface—till the timer goes off.
14. After this is done, gently remove the EasyPress 2 then turn it off.
15. The coaster will be very hot, so you should leave it to get cool before you touch it.

When it is cool, you can peel the design off of it.

CUSTOMIZED DOORMAT

Materials:

- Cricut Machine
- Scrap cardstock (The color does not matter)
- Coir mat (18"x30")
- Outdoor acrylic paint
- Vinyl stencil
- Transfer tape
- Flat round paintbrush
- Cutting mat (12"x24")

Directions:

1. Create your design in Cricut Design Space. You can also download an SVG design of your choice and import it into Cricut Design Space. Make sure that your design is the right size; resize it to ensure that this is so.
2. Next, you are to cut the stencil. You do this by clicking "Make it" in Cricut Design Space when you are done with the design. After this, you select "Cardstock" as the material.

Then, you press the "Cut" button on the Cricut machine.
3. When this is done, remove the stencil from the machine and weed.
4. Next, on the reverse side of the stencil, apply spray glue. After this, attach the stencil to the doormat, exactly where you want your design to be; then, pick up the letter bits left on the cutting mat and glue them to their places in the stencil on the doormat.
5. The next step is to mask the parts of the doormat which you do not want to paint on. You can do this using painters' plastic.
6. Now, it's time to spray-paint your stencil on the doormat. Keeping the paint can about 5 inches away from the doormat, spray up and down, keeping the can pointed straight through the stencil. If it is at an angle, the paint will get under the stencil and ruin your design. Spray the entire stencil 2-3 times to make sure that you do not miss any part and that the paint is even.
7. You're just about done! Now, remove the masking plastic and the stencil and leave the doormat for about one hour to get dry.

T-SHIRTS (VINYL, IRON ON)

Materials:

- Cricut Machine
- T-shirt
- Iron on or heat transfer vinyl
- Fine point blade and light grip mat
- Weeding tools
- EasyPress (regular household iron works fine too, with a little extra work)
- Small towel and Parchment paper

Directions:

1. In preparing for this project, Cricut recommends that you prewash the cloth without using any fabric softener before applying the iron-on or heat transfer vinyl on it. Ensure that your T-shirt is dry and ready before you proceed.
2. On Cricut Design Space, create your design or import your SVG as described in the section on importing images.
3. If you are using an SVG file, select it and click on "Insert Images." When you do this, the

image will appear in the Design Space canvas area.
4. Then, you need to resize the image to fit the T-shirt. To do this, select all the elements, then set the height and width in the edit panel area, or simply drag the handle on the lower right corner of the selection.
5. After this is done, select all the layers and click "Attach" at the bottom of the "Layers" panel, so that the machine cuts everything just as it is displayed on the canvas area.
6. You can preview your design using Design Space's templates. You access this by clicking the icon called "templates" on the left panel of Design Space's canvas. There, you can choose on what surface to visualize your design. Choose the color of your vinyl and the T-shirt so you can see how it will look once completed.
7. Once you are satisfied with the appearance of your design, click "Make It." If you have not connected your machine, you will be prompted to do so.
8. When the "Prepare" page shows, there is a "Mirror" option on the left panel. Ensure that you turn this on. This will make the machine cut it in reverse, as the top is the

part that goes on to the T-shirt. Click "Continue."

9. Next, you are to select the material. When using the Cricut Maker, you will do this in Cricut Design Space. Choose "Everyday Iron-On." On Cricut Explore Air, you select the material using the smart set dial **on the machine**. Set this dial to "Iron-On."

10. Now, it's time to cut. To cut vinyl (and other such light materials), you should use the LightGrip blue mat. Place the iron-on vinyl on the mat with the dull side facing up. Ensure that there are no bubbles on the vinyl; you can do this using the scraper.

11. Install the fine point blade in the Cricut machine, then load the mat with the vinyl on it by tapping the small arrow on the machine. Then, press the "make it" button. When the machine is done cutting the vinyl, Cricut Design Space will notify you. When this happens, unload the mat.

12. With the cutting done, it is time to weed. This must be done patiently so that you do not cut out the wrong parts. Therefore, you should have the design open as a guide.

13. After weeding, it is finally time to transfer the vinyl to the T-shirt. Before this, ensure that

you have prewashed the T-shirt without fabric softener, as mentioned at the beginning of this project.

14. To transfer the design, you can use the EasyPress or a regular pressing iron. Using a pressing iron may be a little more difficult, but it is certainly doable. Before you transfer, ensure that you have the EasyPress mat or a towel behind the material on which you want to transfer the design to allow the material to be pressed harder against the heat.

15. Set the EasyPress to the temperature recommended on the Cricut heat guide for your chosen heat-transfer material and base material. For a combination of iron-on vinyl and cotton, the temperature should be set to 330°F. After preheating the EasyPress, get rid of wrinkles on the T-shirt and press the EasyPress on it for about 5 seconds. Then, place the design on the T-shirt and apply pressure for 30 seconds. After this, apply the EasyPress on the back of the T-shirt for about 15 seconds.

16. If you're using a pressing iron, the process is similar; only that you need to preheat the iron to max heat and place a thin cloth on the design, such that the iron does not have

direct contact with the design or the T-shirt. This will prevent you from burning the T-shirt.
17. Wait for the design to cool off a bit, then peel it off while it is still a little warm.
18. Ensure that you wait for at least 24 hours after this before washing the T-shirt. When you do wash it, be sure to dry it inside out. Also, do not bleach the T-shirt.

3D PAPER FLOWERS (PAPER)

Materials:

- Cricut Machine
- Cricut mat
- Colored scrapbook paper
- Hot glue gun and glue sticks

Directions:

1. To make flowers, you need an appropriate shape for the petals. To make such a shape, you can combine three ovals of equal size. To create an oval, select the circle tool, then create a circle. Then click the unlock button at the bottom of the shape. Once this is

done, you can reshape the circle to form an oval.
2. Duplicate this oval twice and rotate each duplicate a little, keeping the bottom at the same point, as shown in the picture.
3. Select all three ovals and weld them together to get your custom petal shape. For each large flower, you need 12 petals – each one about 3 inches long, while for each small flower, you need 8 petals – each one about 2 inches long. For each flower, you also need a circle shape for the base of about the same width as each petal. Arrange the petals and base circle shape in Cricut Design Studio.
4. Set your material to cardstock on Design Space or the machine, depending on your machine, then cut the petals out.
5. After you cut out the petals, remove them and cut a slit about half an inch long at the bottom of each one. Place a bit of glue on the left side and glue the right side over the glue for each petal.
6. The next thing to do is to place the petals on the circle base. For large flowers, you need three circles of four petals each. For small flowers, you need five circles on the outside and three on the inside. Put a bit of hot glue

on the petal and add to the circle as described above.
7. For the center of the flowers, search Cricut Access for "flower" and chose shapes with several small petals. Cut these out using a different color of cardstock and glue to the center of the flowers.

LUMINARIES

Materials:

- Luminary Graphic (From a Cricut Project)
- Sugar Skull (SVG File)
- Cricut Explore Air or Cricut Maker
- Cardstock Sampler
- Scoring Stylus
- Glue Stick
- Battery-Operated Tea Light

Directions:

1. The first step is to open your Luminary graphic on the Design Space.
2. Then go ahead to upload the SVG file of your Sugar Skull and adjust its size to around 3.25" high. After doing that, move the Sugar Skull

to the bigger part of the Luminary graphic (in the middle of the two score lines) and center-align it.
3. Select the Sugar Skull and the Luminary Graphic and then go ahead and click on "Weld."
4. Try selecting every graphic on the Design Space and click on "Attach." Then copy and paste the selected graphics on the same page (duplication).
5. Select "Make It" at the topmost right-hand corner and then ensure everything is positioned correctly. Click on "Continue." If you notice the files being cut on two different mats, just move them back together on one single mat by simply clicking on these three dots located at the graphic corner.
6. Select "Light Cardstock" under the "Materials" menu, and then start loading the Mat and Cut. Also, ensure that your Scoring Stylus is in Clamp A. This will automatically change your machine settings from scoring to cutting.
7. When the cut-out is done, fold it along the Score lines. Then start gluing the small Flap to the interior part of the lantern's back.
8. Switch on the Battery-Operated Tea Light

and then place your lantern on top of it.

SHAMROCK EARRINGS

Materials

- Cricut Maker
- Earring (from a Cricut Project)
- Rotary Wheel
- Knife Blade
- Fabric Grip Mat
- Strong Grip Mat
- Weeder Tool
- Cricut Leather
- Scraper Tool
- Adhesive
- Pebbled-Faux Leather
- Earring Hooks

Directions

1. First, open the Cricut Project (Earring). You can now either click on "Make It" or "Customize" to edit it.
2. Once you've selected one, click on "Continue."
3. Immediately the Cut page pops up, select

your material and wait for the "Load" tools and Mat to appear.
4. Make your Knife blade your cutting tool in clamp B. This will be used on the Leather.
5. On the StrongGrip Mat, place the Leather and make sure it's facing down. Then load the belt into the machine and press the "Cut" indicator button. When the scoring has been done, go back to the cutting tool and change it to Rotary Wheel so that you can use it on the Faux Leather.
6. Similarly, place your Faux leather on your Fabric Grip Mat, facing down. Next, load the carpet into the machine and tap the "Cut" flashing button.
7. Take away all the items on the Mat with your Scraper tool. Be careful with the small fringes, though.
8. Make a hole in the top circle by making use of the Weeder tool. Make sure the hole is large enough to make the Earring hooks fit in.
9. If necessary, you may have to twist the hook's end with the pliers to fit them in.
10. Close them up after you have looped them inside the hole that was made inside the Earring.

11. Finally, you should glue the Shamrock to the surface of the Earring with adhesive. Wait for it to dry before using it.

VALENTINE'S DAY CLASSROOM CARDS

Materials

- Cricut Maker
- Card Designs (Write Stuff Coloring)
- Cricut Design Space
- Dual Scoring Wheel
- Pens
- Cardstock
- Crayons
- Shimmer Paper

Directions

1. Open the Card Designs (Write Stuff Coloring) on the Design Space, and then click on "Make it" or "Customize" to make edits.
2. When all the changes have been done, Cricut will request you to select a material. Select Cardstock for the Cards and Shimmer Paper for the Envelopes.
3. Cricut will send you a notification when you

need to change the pen colors while creating the Card, and then it will start carving the Card out automatically.
4. You will be prompted later to change the blade because of the Double Scoring Wheel. It is advisable to use the Double Scoring Wheel with Shimmer Paper; they both work best together.
5. When the scoring has been finished, replace the Scoring Wheel with the previous blade.
6. After that, fold the flaps at the Score lines in the direction of the paper's white side, and then attach the Side Tabs to the exterior of the Bottom Tab by gluing them together.
7. You may now write "From:" and "To:" before placing the Crayons into the Slots.
8. Place the Cards inside the Envelopes and tag them with a sharp object.

GLITTER AND FELT HAIR BOW SUPPLIES

Materials

- Hair bow project file in Cricut Design Space
- Cricut Felt
- Glitter Iron-on Vinyl
- Hair Clips (large and small)

- Cricut Mat
- Glue Gun
- Scissors and Weeding tools
- EasyPress

Directions

1. To start, in Cricut Design Space, open the design (hair bow); then, click "Make it now." Should you wish to make changes to the design, click "Customize."
2. Insert a regular blade into the Cricut machine. Then place the materials and the appropriate board on the Cricut mat.
3. Send the document to the Cricut machine and cut it out.
4. After the Cricut machine has cut out the felt and the iron-on, remove the excess vinyl, then cut around each of the bows using scissors.
5. Heat your EasyPress. For the appropriate settings, check the EasyPress Guide.
6. Place the vinyl on the cut-out felt, sticky side down, then heat with the EasyPress for 10 seconds. For larger pieces, do this for each section one at a time, after which you should smooth the EasyPress over the entire design.

7. Remove the transfer paper and repeat this for all the other bows.
8. Use the glue to stick one side of the bigger bow piece (without the sharp edges) to the other side. This will form a circle.
9. Apply glue on the inside and in the middle of that bow piece. After this, fold the piece so that it forms a bow.
10. Stick the bow to its back piece.
11. Fold the small bow piece to the middle of the bow. Fold it in the back and glue it also.
12. Glue the bow to the bigger or smaller bow clips to have your bow.

HALLOWEEN T-SHIRT

Materials

- T-shirt Blanks
- Glam Halloween SVG Files
- Cardstock
- Transfer Sheets (Black and Pink)
- Butcher Paper (comes with Infusible Ink rolls)
- LightGrip Mat
- EasyPress (12" x 10" size recommended)
- EasyPress Mat

- Lint Roller

Directions

1. Import the SVG files into Cricut Design Space and arrange them as you want them on the T-shirt.
2. Change the sizes of the designs to get them to fit on the T-shirt.
3. Using the slice tool, slice the pink band away from the hat's bowler part (the largest piece). Make a copy of this band, and then slice it from the lower part of the hat. With these done, you have three pieces that fit together.
4. You can change the designs' colors as you would like them. When you are done with the preparation, click "Make It."
5. Ensure that you invert your image using the "Mirror" toggle. This is even more important if there is text on your design, as infusible ink designs should be done in inverse. This is because the part with the ink is to go right on the destination material.
6. Click on "Continue"
7. For the material. Select Infusible ink. After this, cut the design out using your Cricut Machine.

8. With the designs cut out, weed the transfer sheet.
9. Cut around the designs such that the transfer tape does not cover any part of the infusible ink sheet. Ensure that this is done well, as any part of the infusible ink that is not in contact with the fabric will not be transferred.
10. Preheat your EasyPress to 385 degrees, and set your EasyPress mat.
11. Prepare your T-shirt by placing it on the EasyPress mat, then using a lint roller to remove any lint from the front.
12. Insert the Cardstock in the t-shirt, just where the design will be between the front and back. That's going to protect the other side of the T-shirt from having the Infusible Ink on it.
13. If necessary, use the lint roller on the T-shirt again, after which you should heat your shirt with the EasyPress. Do this at 385 degrees for 15 seconds.
14. Turn the part where the design faces on the T-shirt. Place the butcher paper on the design, ensuring that the backing does not overlap the design again.
15. Place the EasyPress over the design, and hold it in place for 40 seconds. Do not move the

EasyPress around so that your design does not end up looking smudged.
16. Remove the EasyPress from the shirt and remove the transfer sheet.
17. To layer colors, ensure that your cutting around the transfer sheet is done as close as possible, then repeat the previous three steps for each color. This will prevent the transfer sheet from removing part of the color on the previously transferred design.

HAND LETTERED CAKE TOPPER

Materials

- Glitter Card Stock
- Gold Paper Straw
- Cutting Mat
- Hot Glue Gun

Directions

1. Create your design in Cricut Design Space, or download your desired design and import it into Cricut Design Space using the Direction and click on the "Tips" section.
2. Resize the design as required.

3. Click the "Make it" button.
4. Select Glitter card stock as your material in Design Space and set the dial on your Cricut machine to "Cust."".
5. Place the glitter card stock on your Cutting Mat and load it into the Cricut machine.
6. When this is done, press the "Cut" button on your Cricut machine.
7. After the machine is done cutting the design, remove it from the mat. That can be done much faster by using the Cricut Spatula tool.
8. Finally, using hot glue, stick cut out design to the Gold Paper Straw and stick it in the cake and the photograph.

UNICORN FREE PRINTABLE

Materials

- Printable
- White Card Stock
- Cricut Mat
- Crepe Paper Streamers (varied colors)
- Gold Straws
- Glue Stick
- Hot Glue Gun
- Scissors

Directions

1. Upload the printable image to Cricut Design Space by following the Directions below in this book's "Advice" section.
2. Size the PNG image and expand it to 5.
3. Use your Cricut machine to cut off the head of the unicorn using white cardboard. As well, print and cut out the "stickers."
4. Once you have cut the pieces, glue the horn and other elements using the glue stick.
5. In every color, cut strips of crepe paper about 2" wide; Next, cut each ribbon in three.
6. On the back of the unicorn head, glue the bands on the back edge (of the head), then glue on the top with the horn. Make sure that only half the length of each band is on this site because you will stick the other half on the opposite face of the unicorn head. Flip the head of the unicorn and glue the crepe strips into place.
7. Flip the head one more time and use hot glue to glue the golden paper straw on the underside of the unicorn's head to use as party accessories.

CUSTOM BACK TO SCHOOL SUPPLIES

Materials

- Vinyl
- Standard Grip Mat
- White Paper
- Markers (including black)
- Pencil Case
- 3 Ring Binder
- IPad Pro (optional)
- Apple Pencil
- Cricut Design Space App
- Drawing app (e.g. ProCreate)
- ProCreate Brushes

Directions

1. You need to conversion first of our kid's drawings into an SVG file that Cricut Design Space recognizes. This will be done by tracing it in the ProCreate app.
2. Get your child's design – it should not be too complex, o minimizes weeding.
3. Open the ProCreate app on your iPad.
4. Create a new canvas on ProCreate. Click on the wrench icon and select "IMAGE".

5. Click "TAKE A PHOTO". Take a picture of the design. When you are happy with the image, click "Use it".
6. Add a new layer by clicking the plus sign on the Layer Panel (the two squares icon).
7. From the layer pane, select the layer that contains it the picture and click the N. Also, reduce the layer's opacity so that you can easily see your draw lines.
8. From your imported brushes, select the Marker brush. To avoid the need to import a brush, choose the inking brush. You can resize the brush in the brush settings under the "General" option.
9. On the new layer, trace over the drawing.
10. Click on the wrench icon, click "Share", then "PNG".
11. Next, save the image to your device.
12. Alternately, use your black marker and trace the drawing on a blank piece of paper, then capture a photo with your iPad or phone.
13. The next stage is to cut the design out in Cricut Design Space
14. Open up the Cricut Design Space app on your iPad.
15. Create a new project.
16. Select "Upload" (located at the screen's

bottom). Select "Select from Camera Roll" and select the PNG image you created in ProCreate or the image you traced out.
17. Follow the next steps.
18. Save the design as a cut file and insert it into the canvas. Here, you can resize the design or add other designs.
19. Next, click "Make It" to send it to your Cricut.
20. Choose "Vinyl" as the material.
21. Place the vinyl on the mat and use the Cricut to cut it.
22. Now, you can place the vinyl cutouts on the back-to-school supplies to make your child stand out!

TASSELS

Materials

1. 12" x 18" fabric rectangles
2. Fabric mat
3. Glue gun
4. *Directions*
5. Open Cricut's design area and create your own project.
6. Select the "Image" button in the lower left-

hand corner and search "tassel."
7. Select the image of a rectangle with lines on each side and click "Insert."
8. Place the fabric on the cutting mat.
9. Send the design to the Cricut.
10. Remove the fabric from the mat, saving the extra square.
11. Place the fabric face down and begin rolling tightly, starting on the uncut side. Untangle the fringe as needed.
12. Use some of the scrap fabric and a hot glue gun to secure the tassel at the top.
13. Decorate whatever you want with your new tassels!

MONOGRAMMED DRAWSTRING BAG

Materials

1. Two matching rectangles of fabric
2. Needle and thread
3. Ribbon
4. Heat transfer vinyl
5. Cricut EasyPress or iron
6. Cutting mat
7. Weeding tool or pick
8. *Directions*

9. Open Cricut's design area and create your own project.
10. Select the "Image" button in the lower left-hand corner and search "monogram."
11. Select the monogram of your choice and click "Insert."
12. Place the iron-on material shiny liner side down on the cutting mat.
13. Send the design to the Cricut.
14. Use the weeding tool or pick to remove excess material.
15. Remove the monogram from the mat.
16. Center the monogram on your fabric, then move it a couple of inches down to not be folded up when the ribbon is drawn.
17. Iron the design onto the fabric.
18. Place the two rectangles together, with the outer side of the fabric facing inward.
19. Sew around the edges, leaving a seam allowance.
20. Leave the top open and stop a couple of inches down from the top.
21. Fold the top of the bag down until you reach your stitches.
22. Sew along the lower side of the bent edge, leaving the sides open.
23. Turn the bag right side out.

24. Thread the ribbon through the loop around the top of the bag.
25. Use your new drawstring bag to carry what you need

PAW PRINT SOCKS

Materials

- Socks
- Heat transfer vinyl
- Cutting mat
- Scrap cardboard
- Weeding tool or pick
- Cricut EasyPress or iron

Directions

1. Open Cricut's design area and create your own project.
2. Select the "Image" button in the lower left-hand corner and search "paw prints."
3. Select the paw prints of your choice and click "Insert."
4. Place the iron-on material on the mat.
5. Send the design to the Cricut.
6. Use the weeding tool or pick to remove

excess material.
7. Remove the material from the mat.
8. Fit the scrap cardboard inside of the socks.
9. Place the iron-on material on the bottom of the socks.
10. Use the Easy Press for application on the iron.
11. After cooling, remove the cardboard from the socks.
12. Wear your cute paw print socks!

NIGHT SKY PILLOW

Materials

- Black, dark blue, or dark purple fabric
- Heat transfer vinyl in gold or silver
- Cutting mat
- Polyester batting
- Weeding tool or pick
- Cricut EasyPress

Directions

1. Decide the shape you want for your pillow, and cut two matching shapes out of the fabric.

2. Open Cricut's design area and create your own project.
3. Select the "Image" button in the lower left-hand corner and search
4. "stars."
5. Select the stars of your choice and click "Insert."
6. Place the iron-on material on the mat.
7. Send the design to the Cricut.
8. Use the weeding tool or pick to remove excess material.
9. Remove the material from the mat.
10. Place the iron-on material on the fabric.
11. Select Easy Press to apply it to your iron-on material.
12. Sew the two fabric pieces together, leaving allowance for a seam and a small space open.
13. Fill the pillow with polyester batting through the small open space.
14. Sew the pillow shut.
15. Cuddle up to your starry pillow!

CLUTCH PURSE

Materials

- Two fabrics, one on the outside and one on the outside, for the Fusible interior fleece
- Fabric cutting mat
- D-ring
- Sew-on snap
- Lace
- Zipper
- Sewing machine
- Fabric scissors
- Keychain or charm of your choice

Directions

1. Open Cricut's design area and create your own project.
2. Select the "Image" button in the lower left-hand corner and search for "essential wallet."
3. Select the essential wallet template and click "Insert."
4. Place the fabric on the mat.
5. Send the design to the Cricut.
6. Remove the fabric from the mat.
7. Attach the fusible fleecing to the wrong side of the exterior fabric.
8. Attach lace to the edges of the exterior fabric.
9. Assemble the D-ring strap.

10. Place the D-ring onto the strap and sew it into place.
11. Fold the pocket pieces wrong side out over the top of the zipper, and sew it into place.
12. Fold the pocket's wrong side in and sew the sides.
13. Sew the snap onto the pocket.
14. Position the pocket on the right side of the main tissue lining so that the corners of the pocket's bottom are behind the curved edges of the lining fabric. Sew the lining piece to the zipper tape.
15. Fold the lining behind the pocket and iron in place.
16. Stitch on the opposite side of the snap.
17. Trim the zipper so that it's not overhanging the edge.
18. Sew the two pocket layers to the exterior fabric across the bottom.
19. Sew around all of the layers.
20. Trim the edges with fabric scissors.
21. Turn the clutch almost completely inside out and sew the opening closed.
22. Turn the clutch inside out and press the corners into place.
23. Attach your charm or keychain to the zipper.
24. Carry your new clutch wherever you need it!

ETCHED MONOGRAMMED GLASS

Materials

- A glass of your choice – make sure that the spot you want to monogram is smooth
- Vinyl
- Cutting mat
- Weeding tool or pick
- Glass etching cream

Directions

1. Open Cricut's design area and create your own project.ect the "Image" button in the Design Panel and search for
2. "monogram."
3. Choose your favorite monogram and click "Insert."
4. Place your vinyl on the cutting mat.
5. Send the design to your Cricut.
6. Use a weeding tool or pick to remove the monogram, leaving the vinyl around it.
7. Remove the vinyl from the mat.
8. Carefully apply the vinyl around your glass, making it as smooth as possible, particularly around the monogram.

9. If you have any letters with holes in your monogram, carefully reposition those cutouts in their proper place.
10. Following the Direction, the etching cream, apply it to your monogram.
11. Remove the cream and then the vinyl.
12. Give your glass a good wash.

LIVE, LOVE, LAUGH GLASS BLOCK

Materials

- Glass block
- Frost spray paint
- Clear enamel spray
- Holographic vinyl
- Vinyl transfer tape
- Cutting mat
- Weeding tool or pick
- Fairy lights

Directions

1. Spray the entire glass block with frost spray paint, and let it dry.
2. Spray the glass block with a coat of clear enamel spray, and let it dry.

3. Open Cricut's design area and create your own project.
4. Select the "Text" button in the Design Panel.
5. Type "Live Love Laugh" in the text box.
6. Use the dropdown box to select your favorite font.
7. Arrange the words to sit on top of each other.
8. Place your vinyl on the cutting mat.
9. Send the design to your Cricut.
10. Use a weeding tool or pick to remove the excess vinyl from the design.
11. Apply transfer tape to the design.
12. Remove the paper backing and apply the words to the glass block.
13. Smooth down the design and carefully remove the transfer tape.
14. Place fairy lights in the opening of the block, leaving the battery pack on the outside.

UNICORN WINE GLASS

Materials

1. Stemless wine glasses
2. Outer vinyl in any color you wish.
3. Vinyl transfer tape
4. Cutting mat

5. Weeding tool or pick
6. Very thin glitter in the color of your glitter Mod Podge
7. *Directions*
8. Open Cricut's design area and create your own project.
9. Select the "Text" button in the Design Panel.
10. Type "It's not drinking alone if my unicorn is here."
11. Using the dropdown box, select your favorite font.
12. Adjust the positioning of the letters, rotating some to give a whimsical look.
13. Select the "Image" button on the Design Panel and search for
14. "unicorn."
15. Select your favorite unicorn and click "Insert," then arrange your design how you want it on the glass.
16. Place your vinyl on the cutting mat, making sure it is smooth and making full contact.
17. Send the design to your Cricut.
18. Use a weeding tool or pick to remove the excess vinyl from the design. Use the Cricut BrightPad to help if you have one.
19. Apply transfer tape to the design, pressing firmly and making sure there are no bubbles.

20. Remove the paper backing and apply the words to the glass where you'd like them. Let at least a few inches at the bottom for the glitter.
21. Smooth down the design and carefully remove the transfer tape.
22. Coat the bottom of the glass in Mod Podge, wherever you would like glitter to be. Give the area a wavy edge.
23. Sprinkle glitter over the Mod Podge, working quickly before it dries.
24. Add another layer of Mod Podge and glitter, and set it aside to dry.
25. Cover the glitter in a thick coat of Mod Podge.
26. Allow the glass to cure for at least 48 hours.

WOODEN SIGN

Materials

- Vinyl – you can choose the color
- Transfer tape
- Cricut tools kit
- Your wood backing

Directions

1. Stage one is to prepare the wood. How far it takes is up to you what type of finished product you are after.
2. If you want the wood to be rough, then you just need to cut it to shape with a jigsaw.
3. If you are searching for a smooth finish, then you need to sand it several times first. You may also want to varnish or paint the wood.
4. You can now design your phrase or image on Cricut design space. You need to make sure it is the right size for your wood!
5. It is important to tell the machine to cut out white space between any letters; you only want the words.
6. If the writing is bigger than your cutting mat you need to include an easy-to-cut breakpoint. An alternative color square is usually a good option.
7. Print the phrase or image on your Cricut machine. It will advise you if more material needs to be added.
8. You'll need to use your wedding tool to make sure the edges are exactly how you want them.
9. Carefully apply transfer tape to the other side of your letters. The letters should be lined up

exactly how you want them to look on the sign.
10. You can then peel off the backing, and the letters should stay attached to the transfer tape.
11. Then you should be able to apply this directly to the wood. The transfer tape should come off;
12. That's it; Now you got to do it! Hang it!

NAIL ART

Materials

- Vinyl
- Nail polish – your color of choice
- Topcoat – to make the polish and nail art last longer.

Directions

1. Again, you need to take a look at the Cricut Design Space and create the design that you want to appear on your nails.
2. There is virtually no limit to the design you can create!
3. Place a piece of vinyl into your Cricut

machine and send the design to the machine. It will cut the intricate shapes for you.
4. You need to make sure they are the right size for your nails.
5. You could use glue to attach the vinyl but this could leave you in a mess! Start by placing the design on your nail and removing any excess vinyl.
6. You can then paint over it with your topcoat. This will hold the vinyl in place.
7. The alternative is to hold the design in place and paint the nail a different color. The design will be left unpainted; all you have to do is carefully remove the vinyl. Again, a topcoat should be added to protect the art on your nail.

DAD JOKE VINYL T-SHIRT

Materials

- Your Favorite White Shirt
- Cricut Creator (or any other automated cutting machines using SVG files) or Discover Air 2 Cutting Machine
- Iron-On (Vinyl energy transfer) in different shades (Expressions of Cricut Vinyl)

- Instruments for weeding (Amazon Cricut)
- Easy Press 2 and Mat

Directions

1. To keep do it making the "Dad Jokes?" I guess you're asking about RAD jokes! Hat, open Cricut Machine Space (or other device software), and append an SVG image.
2. Drop the imported picture onto a new canvas, size it to fit the shirt (we recommend making it around 10 "long for the shirt of a mature male), and in the upper right corner, click the green" Print it Now "icon."
3. To remove the iron-on vinyl with the grinding machine, the remaining vinyl is scraped off using the weeding equipment.
4. Next, in the Online Quick reference source, use Easy Press 2 to apply the template to the top, observing the time and temperature configuration needed. Short, quick, and completely enjoyable! That will give Dad a great present for Father's Day, Christmas, Birthdays, and more!
5. This approach even performed on a hat very well! Use your Sport Flex Iron-On adhesive or Infusible Ink and Easy Press

Miniature on this polyester trucking cover for a super fun gift idea.

FATHER'S DAY COFFEE TRAY GIFT

Materials

- Acrylic Spray Paints
- Wooden Plate, Wood Plate
- Device for Weeding
- Tape Move
- Mat Cutting
- Vinyl Oramask Stencil
- Paintbrush or Sponge
- (I used the Cricut Maker) Cutting System

Directions:

1. In the Design Room, import the design you're using and resize it to suit your breakfast tray. You may either pick or move the concept to size or manually insert the measurements in the width and length boxes.
2. Then pick your content from the drop-down list by pressing the make its icon. I used the silkscreen glitter setting on my Cricut Creator, and it functioned well.

3. With the bottom side facing upwards, put the stencil content on the cutting mat, and load the mat into the unit. Verify that all the settings are right and then click the start button that flashes.
4. Using a hooked tool to root away from the characters that create a stencil after slicing is full. Make sure that the letter centers remain in place.
5. Cut a piece of parchment paper to size and burnish well around the whole stencil with a scraper kit.
6. Peel the tape away from the document backrest and the Oramask. Place it down immediately and brush through it again if any bits do not adhere to the parchment paper.
7. To apply firm pressure on the whole pattern, focus the stencil on the plate and use the separator tool once more. To guarantee a very nice stick, do this many times!
8. Then, by beginning at the corner and peeling at an angle, peel away the transfer tape.
9. To dab acrylic paint on the stencil, use a sponge dauber or a dry paintbrush. Compared to a brushing action, I prefer to use a pouncing motion to prevent the paint

from seeping except under the edges that might not be completely pinned down.
10. To expose the crisp, clean paint lines, let the paint dry entirely and then gently peel away the stencil vinyl.
11. To detach the smaller bits of vinyl from within the messages, use the hook method once again.
12. To cover up the corners, use a wet information brush if you have any places that have leaked. This is all that there is to it!
13. This will make a new mother the right basis for a gift package. Then leave it at the door and make her day! Fill it with cute coffee mugs, coffee beans, local jams, and freshly baked croissants.

MAKING BIG SPIDERS

Materials

- Gun Quick Glue
- Creator Cricut
- Blades of Rotary
- Thought Cricut
- Mat Cloth

Directions

1. I began by making a felt table runner with a spider. With the Cricut Creator and rotary cutter, you can use any sort of felt, but I have considered the Cricut felt sheet to become the best for not having lint behind with the mat.
2. At Cricut Design Room, I built a template for two separate wide spider nets.
3. Related: How to use pictures in Cricut Space Architecture
4. Open the file Template Space and press the Create It button in grey. Select two project copies when you get to the pad overview, then press Request. Choose Begin.
5. Select 2 Copies of the Project
6. From the cut computer, pick your Cricut Creator. From the materials collection, pick Felt. Click Edit Software to encourage you to click a Rotary Blade.
7. Using Cricut Creator to pick rotary edge to cut felt.
8. Using the Cricut Tool to cut out all the felt. You would have tall small spider webs, two small spider's webs, and two little red circles when you are done.

9. Split felt utilizing the Cricut Creator.
10. The handled spider web pulls very quickly right off the ground, but on the ground, you are left with a lot of little felt bits. You should use an XL scraper to clean your floor easily. For cardstock, as well, this fits well.
11. Using the XL scraper to wipe up meat scraps
12. Spider Network Noticed
13. Using hot glue to tie the red circles cut out on the giant spider net fragments behind the hourglass.
14. Using hot glue to tie the black spider webs in lines, alternating colors, to the black spider webs. I'm so impressed at how easily the Creator can carve so smoothly and precisely those complicated cuts.

SPIDER BOX LIGHTING

Materials

- Vellum
- Wheel of Scoring
- Adhesive
- Creator Cricut
- Wheel Tip Double Scoring
- Mat Light Grip

- Print Sparkle, Pewter

Directions

1. A spider luminaire was the next project I produced to go on my table. To render a luminary, the sparkle paper is the right glittery stuff.
2. Many great designs instantly pop up if you check for "luminary" in Cricut Design Room.
3. They are crafted so that they are rated and cut. I have found the right spider luminary template because I was looking for a spider's design at this party. To use more of a single sheet of paper, I rendered it as big as I could.
4. Room of Cricut Nature-Spider Luminary
5. Space File for Cricut Design: Spider Luminary
6. Please make sure to pick Sparkle Paper from the list of products. It will show you that the double scoring wheel is needed for you.
7. Load the Cricut Builder Double Scoring Wheel
8. Make sure the tip indicates the .02 on your scoring wheel.
9. Double Scoring Wheel with Cricut
10. Load onto your mat your sparkle file, sparkle

side down. On the back of the document, the computer can produce the score lines.
11. Adaptive tool scheme of Cricut Builder with scoring wheel
12. On the computer, it would then prompt you to use the fine point blade. Shift the razor, and the Vellum is taken off.
13. Before cutting out the spiders, make sure you change the content settings to Vellum.
14. Double score lines on the luminary worm
15. Adhere the Vellum to the luminaire's interior.
16. Apply the Vellum to the luminaire inside,
17. Fold the light on all the lines of the score. You will fold the shimmer sheet with no cracking using the double score row.
18. Assemble the light. To guarantee that the luminaire remains intact, use a good adhesive such as red tape. Since the glitter paper has a shiny, glossy finish, it won't fit standard double-sided adhesive.
19. To assemble the luminaire, use red tape to
20. This scintillating paper is too much fun. In reality, it appears much cooler. Attach to the bottom some sand or tiny rocks, a little LED tea lamp, and your spider lamp is ready to shine.

HALLOWEEN BOARD

Materials

- Extreme Shimmer by Folk-art in black
- Black and white acrylic paint (I used acrylics from Folk-art)
- Explore or Creator Crict
- The Paintbrushes
- 18"x5 "woodwork sign
- Black and Orange Sticky Vinyl
- Tape Move

Directions:

1. I colored an incomplete sign with gold paint in the middle and black from around the frame I bought at Michaels, then replaced the spray paint with Intense Glitter paint in black. In the image, it is hard to tell, but the black edge is very sparkly. Then I attached my Cricut with some vinyl cut out to complete it.
2. Paint the wooden sign first. Paint white for the inner part and black for the outer edge/frame.
3. When the base course of paint is finished,

apply a coat of black Intense Glitter paint (or more if you like it to look glitterier). Set to dry aside.
4. Open the Space File for Halloween Sign Concept.
5. You'll need a big mat because it's bigger than 12, "cut the cabbages out of green, cut the phrases out of black vinyl.
6. To bring the terms and pumpkins onto the dark wood sign, use transfer tape.

HALLOWEEN PUMPKIN VINYL DESIGN

Materials

- Vinyl in your preference of paint
- Transfer Tape
- Cricut Machine
- Simple Pumpkins
- SVG file

Directions

1. Gathering materials. You will need a plain pumpkin, art vinyl (you can pick whatever vinyl and shades you prefer), a Rae Dunn template and use the Vector format

document, a Cricut machine, and a tape transfer (you can need this to apply the tapered text to the pumpkins).
2. Scale the picture according to the pumpkin's size. The picture should be about 4 x 6 inches in dimension.
3. Break the image and weed it (delete the undesirable aspect of the slashed image, eliminate the outside around the letters in this case).
4. When adding to the pumpkin, attach transfer tape to your cut picture to scale and scrape away the transfer tape.

THE UNICORN MASK

Materials

- Cricut machine
- Felt – various colors
- Fabric Glue
- Scissors

Directions

1. You'll need to find a mask image of your unicorn or other animals. This is not

something that already exists in Design Space. You must locate one and upload it to your Cricut Design Space. You need to resize the image according to the size of your head or that of your child.
2. You can select the colors you want for the various parts of the unicorn mask. By pressing "make it" the Cricut will print the different colors, cutting in the process.
3. You can now assemble the parts of the mask, the guide on Design Space should help ensure you get this part right. You can opt to use fabric glue or adhesive fabric and transfer tape to get the different layers together.
4. It is also important to add two holes to your mask. One should be on each side of the mask to allow the ribbon to be threaded through. This is important to ensure the mask can be properly secured.
5. It is also possible to add to the design by using glitter, sequins or embroidering a pattern into it. The choice is yours!

PERSONALIZED WATER BOTTLES

Materials:

- Smooth Outdoor Vinyl Water Bottle
- Transfer Tape Scraper or Brayer Blank Water Bottles

Directions

1. Open Cricut Design Space and design your text, then add a name using an outline. Create a second text box smaller than the first one. Attach these two layers to separate your initial and name and resize to suit your water bottle.
2. To stick the initial name to your water bottle you will use your transfer tape.
3. Carefully peel your transfer tape, and you are done. Even though you used outdoor vinyl, you might still handwash the bottles. This way, you are sure to make them last as long as possible.

FELT ROSES

Materials:

- SVG files with 3D flower design
- Felt Sheets
- Fabric Grip Mat

- Glue Gun

Directions

1. First of all, upload your Flower SVG Graphics into the Cricut Design Space.
2. Create several copies of the flowers, as many as you wish, selecting the colors you want in the Color Sync Panel (by dragging and dropping the images onto the color you would want them to be cut on). Immediately after you're done with that, click on "Make it" on the Cricut design space.
3. Click on "Continue". After your Cricut Maker is connected and registered, under the "materials" options, select "Felt".
4. If your rotary blade is not in the machine, insert it. Following the Fabric Grip Mat, place the first felt sheet (in order of color), then load them into your Cricut Maker. Press the "cut" button when this is done.
5. Apply Hot Glue on the circle right in the middle and press the felt flowers that you rolled up on the glue. Hold this in place and do not let it go until the glue binds it.
6. Wait for the glue to dry, and your roses are ready for use.

GEOMETRIC LAMPSHADE

Materials:

- White cardstock
- Metallic cardstock if you prefer
- Ribbon or string
- Hot glue gun

Directions

1. In Design Space, go into the library and enter the "Make It Now" unit. Find the project labeled "Geo Ball."
2. Once the project loads, place your cardstock on your cutting mat and send it to score the fold lines.
3. Once your paper is scored, glue the metallic and white pieces of paper together. Begin folding the paper to create the geometric shape. Place a line of glue along one edge and bring the project into its final shape.
4. If you are hanging your pendant, make sure to attach your ribbon or string to the bottom of the shape and hang it from your ceiling!

TAKEOUT-STYLE BOXES

Materials:

- Sticker paper for labels or stickers
- Cardstock
- Hot glue gun or glue dots

Directions

1. If you are going to add stickers labels to your boxes, design them in Design Space with the image or text you prefer. Consider adding the title of the event and the date to the label so guests know right away how long they have the leftovers in their fridge. Create various sizes to fit over the cardstock boxes you are about to create or other containers you might need to use.
2. Once your stickers or labels are created, send the file to print and cut.
3. Search the Chinese Take Out Boxes template in the Design Space library and load it into a new workspace. Choose a variety of sizes. Load your cardstock onto your cutting mats and send the file to cut.
4. Fold your cut cardstock along the score lines.

Apply glue along the edges to assemble the box and reinforce the seams.

5. If you are adding stickers to your boxes, add them now. For other containers, keep the stickers nearby or apply them onto them as well. You are ready to send your guests away in style now!

LATTE STENCIL

Materials:

- Cardstock or vellum
- Coffee in a mug and a dusting material

Directions

1. Measure the top of your mugs or your favorite mug that you use often. In Design Space, create a circle or shape that will rest over the lip of your mug and add another small circle to the side of it to be the tab that you will hold while the stencil is in use.
2. Write your message or create your image on your stencil. Make sure to place your image in the center. Send the file to cut on your vellum. Weed the small pieces in the center of

your design and peel away the outside vellum or cardstock you do not need.

3. When your latte is ready and still nice and hot, place the stencil over your mug and dust your favorite topping over it to create the design. Gently lift the stencil away to reveal your barista design. If you used vellum, wash the stencil off and lay it aside to dry for your next coffee creation!

FELT OWLS

Materials:

- Various pinecones washed and air dried
- Felt in various colors like brown, black, white, yellow, and teal
- Hot glue gun
- Ribbon

Directions

1. First, you will want to design the pieces of the owl face and wings in Design Space. The face is made of two large circles attached. The eyes are two-layered circles, and the nose is a teardrop shape. The wings are two-layered

teardrops and can have small circle embellishments. You can also create a stomach piece, which is a circle with small circles inside of it. "Eyebrows" in two wings or a small triangle are also good embellishments to design.
2. Send your images to cut out of your felt. Tape down your felt pieces with masking tape or painter's tape if you want to make sure the fabric does not move around while cutting.
3. Begin creating your pinecone owls by taking the pieces and start gluing them onto the pinecone. Alternate colors and styles to create a little village of owls. Glue a small piece of glue to the top of the pinecones to be able to hang them, if you want, or leave them to sit flat on a surface.

PAPER FLOWER WREATH

Materials:

- Wreath base
- Colored cardstock
- Hot glue gun
- Coordinated fabric, if desired

Directions

1. In Design Space, find a variety of different flower and leaf projects. Aim for about three or four different flower designs that are different in size—various colors and sizes. Follow the directions for compiling the petals and creating the flowers. Pinch the leaves or fold the bottoms over to add dimension to the leaves. A good goal is to have about 30 different flowers and 15 different leaves to start.
2. If you decided to wrap your wreath with fabric, add a little glue to one end from the crown and begin winding it around the crown and securing the other end with hot glue when it is covered. It is not necessary to cover the entirety of the crown with fabric or use it at all. Just make enough flowers and leaves to cover any exposed wreath base that you do not want to be seen.
3. Begin adding your flowers to your wreath with your hot glue gun. Make sure you are mixing shapes and colors on your wreath. Once all the flowers are added to your wreath, fill in with the leaves. Add other

embellishments if you want. When the glue is dry, get ready to hang it.

CRICUT FOIL STREAMERS

Materials

- Cricut party foil in colors of your choice
- Green StandardGrip mat
- Cricut Fine-Point Blade
- Weeding tool
- Scraper tool

Directions:

1. Start a new project in Design Space.
2. Select 'Images' from the left-hand side menu.
3. Search for image
4. M7D2D9CA.
5. Choose 'Square' from the 'Shapes' menu on the left-hand side menu.
6. Click 'Make it.'
7. Position the spiral in the middle of the board to give the Cricut enough cutting room.
8. Cut the party foil to the size of the cutting mat and stick it onto the mat.
9. Use either the brayer or scraping tool to

ensure the foil is smooth and stuck down properly to the mat.
10. Make sure the fine-point blade is loaded into the Cricut.
11. Load the cutting mat with the foil into the Cricut.
12. Set the Cricut dial to custom.
13. In Design Space, click 'Continue.'
14. Select 'Party foil' as the material.
15. **Click 'Continue.'**
16. When the Cricut is ready to cut, click 'Go.'
17. When the Cricut has finished cutting, unload the cutting mat.
18. Carefully remove the excess foil and use the weeding tool to weed the small starts on the foil.
19. Use the spatula to remove the streamer from the cutting mat gently.

FROGGY RAIN GEAR

Materials

- Matching green raincoat and rain boots
- White outdoor vinyl
- Vinyl transfer tape
- Cutting mat

- Weeding tool or pick

Directions

1. Open Cricut's design area and create your own project.
2. Select the "Image" button in the lower left-hand corner and search for "frog."
3. Choose your favorite frog and click "Insert."
4. Copy the frog and resize. You will need three frogs, a larger one for the coat and two smaller ones for each boot.
5. Place your vinyl on the cutting mat.
6. Send the design to your Cricut.
7. Use a weeding tool or pick to remove the excess vinyl from the design.
8. Apply transfer tape to the design.
9. Remove the paper backing and apply the design to the coat or boot.
10. Rub the tape to transfer the vinyl to the rain gear, making sure there are no bubbles. Carefully peel the tape away.
11. Dress your kid up to play in the rain!

SNOWY WREATH

Materials

- Grapevine wreath
- Silver berry stems
- Spray adhesive
- Silver and white glitter
- Piece of wood to fit across the center of the wreath Wood stain, if desired
- Drill and a small bit
- Twine
- White vinyl
- Vinyl transfer tape
- Cutting mat
- Weeding tool or pick

Directions

1. Thread the silver berry stems throughout the grapevine wreath.
2. Use the spray adhesive and glitter to create patches of "snow" on the wreath.
3. If you want to stain your wood, do so now and set it aside to dry.
4. Open Cricut's design area and create your own project.

5. Select the "Text" button in the lower left-hand corner.
6. Choose your favorite font and type, "Let it snow."
7. Place your vinyl on the cutting mat.
8. Send the design to your Cricut.
9. Use a weeding tool or pick to remove the excess vinyl from the text.
10. Apply transfer tape to the words.
11. Remove the paper backing and apply the design to the wood piece.
12. Rub the tape to transfer the vinyl to the wood, making sure there are no bubbles. Carefully peel the tape away.
13. Drill two small holes in the corner of the wood and thread the twine through.
14. Hang your wreath and sign for the winter season!

ANTIQUED KITCHEN SIGN

Materials

1. Wooden sign of the desired size
2. Black and white spray paint
3. Vinyl
4. Vinyl transfer tape

5. Cutting mat
6. Weeding tool or pick
7. *Directions*
8. Paint the sign black and set it aside to dry.
9. Open Cricut's design area and create your own project.
10. Select the "Text" button in the lower left-hand corner.
11. Choose your favorite font and type a phrase for your kitchen sign.
12. See below for some possibilities.
13. **Eat Here**
14. **Marketplace**
15. **Family**
16. **Gather Here**
17. **Diner**
18. Place your vinyl on the cutting mat.
19. Send the design to your Cricut.
20. Use a weeding tool or pick to remove the excess vinyl from the text.
21. Apply transfer tape to the words.
22. Remove the paper backing and apply the design to the sign.
23. Rub the tape to transfer the vinyl to the wood, making sure there are no bubbles. Carefully peel the tape away.
24. Use white spray paint on the whole sign. Do

so messily, leaving some spots of black for the aged appearance. Set aside to dry.
25. After drying, peel away the vinyl letters.
26. Hang your sign and enjoy!

FUN FOAM STAMPS

Materials

- Craft Foam Sheets
- Wooden blocks - small blocks, not larger than 4 inches
- Glue
- Cricut machine

Directions

1. Open your Design Space and go to Images. You can search for the images through the library by using specific words or browse to find the images you like. You can choose letters as well if you would like to make letter stamps. Numbers can be used as well. You can use fun images of unicorns, hearts, stars, or whichever shape or image you find interesting. Use the top editing panel to size the images for your stamps. Images shouldn't

be larger than 2 inches, but you can also make them larger or smaller if you prefer. Make sure to size the images to fit the wooden blocks.

2. Once you click on "Make it", make sure to set the material to cutting foam as you will be using foam sheets for your designs. You can cut several images at once, while it is handy not to have more than 6 x 2-inch images prepared for cutting. Set your cutting mat and arrange your foam material – you can use different colors for different stamp images. Once you get everything in place, you can start cutting. Once the images are cut out, you can start gluing them to the wooden blocks. The glue should be left to dry overnight before you start using stamps. You are all done and good to go!

PERSONALIZED DOORMAT

Materials

- Heavy cardstock
- Doormat – plain
- Stencil brush
- Tape

- Fabric paint
- Cricut machine
- Gloves are recommended since you will be using fabric paint

Directions

1. What is important for you to make for this project is the pattern for your doormat - you can use a cute design or go for a witty statement written in a bold and interesting font. You can also download the SVG file with an already-ready design. If you are uploading the SVG file, you will have fewer steps to complete as you will be able to cut in only a couple of steps.
2. If you are starting from scratch, make sure to create a base element for your design - this would be a layer on which you will place your statement or another cool design. You may select the font of your choice, and in case you are searching for an interesting image, you can always browse through the image library. Once you have the design ready, you must select the layers and click on "Weed". You want to cut and weed the image, then remove the negative part - the negative part would be

the letters inside your design. You will need the letters to be cut out, so you could make a paint pattern for the doormat.

3. Once your design is ready and happy with the outcome, you can click on the "Make it" button to send your design to cut. Make sure to prepare the material and your mat and set the cutting preferences to heavy cardstock. You will use heavy cardstock as your stencil. When the cutting is done, take the tape, the paint and the brush alongside your pattern and let's move onto the finishing step.

4. For the final step, you will carefully glue the edges of the pattern with tape so you can fixate it to the doormat. Take the stencil brush and use it to apply paint over the pattern. Careful not to paint outside the edges of the pattern. Paint over the letters. Let the doormat dry, then remove the pattern and wish your visitors

CONCLUSIONS

You've just become a professional Cricut user! However, it would help if you did not forget the most important things discussed in this book. If you forget things quickly, have this book with you every time you want to work on your Cricut machine.

If you have worked your way through the projects in this book, you are well on your way to becoming a Cricut pro. Like a recipe book, the projects, along with the ideas in this book, can be adjusted, adapted and added to, so that you can make each one uniquely yours.

With the Cricut, you are going to find birthdays, special occasions, seasonal holidays and even school projects to be a lot easier, as well as more personalized.

Everyone loves receiving gifts, cards and so on, that have been designed especially for them.

Since the development of the Amazon platform, more and more people have started to develop their products using Cricut technology. We've all been told to look for products on the Chinese markets, buy massive quantities and get the products at meager prices. Some people prefer to use the Cricut machine to create their decorations, while others can even make some money out of their projects. Just think of customized T-shirts or mugs, as these items are trendy today.

Owning this type of machine is a great opportunity for many people to expand their crafting abilities and it's great if you want to branch out and explore new things as a crafter as well because you can add so many new things to their repertoire. This machine can literally have endless possibilities for a crafter as a result. You can make or you can print on just about anything. For example, if you are a vinyl lover, you could have an endless supply of things that you can put vinyl on such as glasses, mugs and a plethora of other options.

www.ingramcontent.com/pod-product-compliance
Lightning Source LLC
Chambersburg PA
CBHW070900080526
44589CB00013B/1140